big plan

FOR THE CREATIVE MIND

Dannie Fountain & Reina Pomeroy

Copyright © 2017 by Dannie Fountain & Reina Pomeroy

All rights reserved. This book or any portion thereof may not be reproduced or used in any manner whatsoever without the express written permission of the publisher except for the use of brief quotations in a book review.

Printed in the United States of America

First Printing, 2017

ISBN -099931999X

bigplanforthecreativemind.com

To anyone who has ever been told no, this book is for you. Find your path to yes.

– Dannie

To those who dare to dream and make a mark on the world. Life is too damn short not to love every single day.

xo, Reina

Contents

Foreword 7
Introduction 13
1. Tara Gentile, INTP 23
2. Natalie Franke, INFP 35
3. Lacey Sites, INTJ 49
4. Lara Casey, INFP 61
5. Ashley + Graham Scobey, ESTJ + INFP 75
6. Amber McCue, ENTJ 91
7. Reina Pomeroy, ENTJ 107
8. Tara Newman, INFJ 121
9. Courtney Johnston, ENFJ 133
10. Jillian Smith, ESFJ-A 145
11. Jenna Kutcher, ESFP 157
12. Lisa Jacobs, INTJ 167
13. Afterword 179
14. Gratitude 193

Visit **bigplanforthecreativemind.com**
to grab your bonus content!

FOREWORD

Goals. Plans. Time Lines. Commitments.

A*re you feeling antsy-pants and creatively constricted yet?*
I know, I know. I know that feeling WELL, actually. (It's why I'm here.)

If you're anything like me, the thought of setting measurable goals can either inspire or depress you — motivating action and sparking ideas of what's REALLY possible . . . or dredging up a mental search history of benchmarks boldly set (doodled *and* color-coded), then quietly abandoned.

"I'm too creative for this kind of structure. I need flexibility and space for inspiration!" you've cried, quietly envious of #getitdone humans who seem to have NO qualms around chasing goals.

And yet—if you're totally honest—your highest (easily-makes-time-for-five-minutes-of-daily-journaling-and-meditation) self knows this to be true:

ALL humans are creative by nature.

We were designed to expand and grow. It's how the Universe rolls.

It's in our nature to reach. To move. To try new things.

In other words: We were MADE to set goals and take action toward them.

And so, new friend, I have to say (to both of us!), with love and heart emojis:

Your "I can't work like that" story is just an excuse.

And our excuses don't serve us. Or anyone, for that matter.

(Literally. ZERO humans served.)

That's why, excuses aside: **My goal for this foreword is to help you see how THIS VERY BOOK can help you flip the script and rewrite your story around the pursuit of meaningful goals.**

First up, a bit of context.

I'm Nikki Elledge Brown. I first met Reina when she invited me to be a guest on her Creative Empire podcast (still one of my fave interview convos to date).

We got to know each other even better when I hosted a small mastermind for family-focused female entrepreneurs. When she told me the idea for this book, two words came to mind: SO. NEEDED.

Like Reina, among many other things, I'm a military spouse, a mother, a teacher, a speaker, a writer, an entrepreneur, and — YEP — a creator.

Since starting my business in 2013 I've created courses, workshops, communities, partnerships, a podcast, and (SOON) my first book.

Did I mention that I'm also a recovering perfectionist and self-proclaimed creative commitment-phobe?

FOREWORD

That part's important.

My business story is an unconventional one.

I'm one of those entrepreneurs who got to taste game-changing financial success VERY early on.

Long story short-ish: I generated more than $21,000 in revenue in my first six weeks of business when more than 70 amazing entrepreneurs signed up to get my help writing clear, sincere copy for their websites.

In the months that followed, I worked one-on-one with more than 160 small business owners and eventually launched my online program A Course About Copy®, which pushed my revenue to more than $110,000 in my first 10 months of business.

As a former park ranger and part-time college faculty member who was used to averaging less than $15 per hour of work, this was HUGE for me.

So how did it happen?

#goals, friend.

G.O.A.L.S. Plans. Fear. Resistance. And focused ACTION.

To be honest, the scale of my initial "boom" was completely unplanned and unexpected. When I first dreamed of how I could use my communication skills to serve entrepreneurs, I thought it would be cool to make $20K in a YEAR. I never expected it to happen in less than two months.

But that $100K milestone? *That was intentional AF.*

Toward the end of that first year as I tipped over my first $50K in total revenue I remember thinking, "Wouldn't it be cool to make more than $100K in my first year?"

Right around that time my (now) buddy Amber

McCue, whom you'll meet in this book, was hosting her yearly Planathon. I loved her style (and the feeling of declaring our "big kahuna" goals in FB-public) so much that I ended up hiring her to help me create a 90-day plan to launch my course and hit my first year goal.

I ended up procrastinating like a MUG and squishing that 90 days of work into 45-ish instead, but the sheer exercise of making a plan and committing to it was EXACTLY what I needed to quiet the distractions and focus on my mission.

Instead of constricting my creativity, the plan gave me freedom to focus.

For years I focused my creative buns off while riding the entrepreneurial roller coaster.

(You know the one: One minute you're high on life feeling like EVERYTHING IS POSSIBLE, and the next you're doubting if anyone but your mama will open your emails. #creativelivingFTW)

I like to call this phase "biz puberty" because it's awkward, exhilarating, and often uncomfortable.

You may LOOK like you have it all together on the outside, but on the inside you're questioning everything.

You feel compelled to CREATE and yet (if you're honest) you're spinning your wheels.

You resist the blueprints and formulas because they don't feel aligned, yet holding the door open for ALL creative possibilities and opportunities is freaking exhausting.

It's time to try something different.

Eliminate the other options and the temptation to be open to #allthethings right now.

It's time to commit. And yeah, I know. It can be scary.

FOREWORD

For a while, after my second son was born, I resisted making plans in my own business.

I bought into the "ick, goals, constricting!" mindset and convinced myself that by refusing to commit to set goals and plans, I was committing to taking only "ALIGNED and inspired action."

Ultimately I realized that I was actually just committed to being *stuck*. #notsexy

Lesson learned?

We don't have to choose either goals OR creativity.

We can have both. This book will show you how.

So here's your mission, should you choose to accept it:

If you're not 100% satisfied with the direction and momentum of your life and work right now, give yourself permission to try something different.

Use the ideas in this book to set goals and make plans you feel INSPIRED by.

Bake in flexibility and room to pivot as you go.

Choose your own planning adventure and COMMIT to making your magic.

In the words of W.H. Murray:

"Until one is committed, there is hesitancy, the chance to draw back, always ineffectiveness. Concerning all acts of initiative (and creation), there is one elementary truth, the ignorance of which kills countless ideas and splendid plans: that the moment one definitely commits oneself, then **Providence moves too***."*

Let's go move some Providence, shall we?

To the big plan for YOUR creative mind,
Nikki

Nikki Elledge Brown
Creator, *Naptime Empires*™ and *A Course About Copy*®
ESFJ
@nikkielledgebrown
Houston, Texas

INTRODUCTION

Goal Setting Really Is For You

"It's not about 'what can I accomplish?' but 'what do I want to accomplish?' Paradigm shift."
— BRENÉ BROWN

Why We Wrote This Book

As creative entrepreneurs, we have so much to offer the world. We have skills and talents that far exceed the world's wildest imaginations, but perhaps more importantly, we have a purpose that's rooted to our core and drives us forward beyond barriers each and every single day.

Just because we are more creative, more right-brained, more flow- or intuition-oriented than our corporate peers, doesn't mean that we shouldn't be setting plans. In fact, we have the freedom to plan differently — the chance to set our intentions in a more meaningful way.

But how do we get to a place where we're goal setting and planning for our businesses, in a way that is more meaningful than just a modified corporate structure? Do a quick Google search for "goal setting" and you'll find corporate-style, linear, left-brain books on the topic. Many creative individuals and people who want a little bit more flow to life get turned off by this. We're thinking about life in a way that doesn't really match up with the left-brain, linear type of planning. We start to feel lost. Perhaps in the past, in our corporate job or left-brain-dominant environment, we've been told that our process is wrong. This free-flowing sort of thinking was deemed inadequate or otherwise "less than" the traditional left-brain way of doing things.

This simply isn't the case. We're firm believers in the idea that **there is more than one way to do something and goal setting is no exception**. But here's the thing: We also think that goal setting is non-negotiable. It doesn't matter how you do it, just that you *are doing it*. A Harvard Business School study conducted in 1979 revealed remarkable statistics relating to goal setting and success: 83% of the population does not have goals; 14% have a plan in mind, but goals are unwritten; and 3% have goals written down. The study found that the 14% who have goals are 10 times more successful than those without goals. The 3% with written goals are three times more successful than the 14% with unwritten goals. Writing your goals down sets you up to be exponentially more successful. All it took was pen to paper!

In the creative industry there are plenty of tools like PowerSheets™, the Conquer Kit, Your Best Year, or the Fresh Start Notebook breaking the mold of the standard goal setting book. These leaders are writing and creating content around these topics and helping creatives get their minds around what it is they could/should be doing to have a mindful business. What we fail to see is a singular place where where all of these unique goal setting strategies, mindset, and execution are being showcased.

How to Use This Book

Have you ever been to Cici's Pizza? Once inside, you grab a plate, and you can pick any of a variety of different slices of pizza. You could pick one pepperoni, one Hawaiian, and one supreme to make up your meal for that day. It's more fun and satisfying than eating three slices of pepperoni, we think.

We believe goal setting should be the same. You are an individual with unique skillsets and needs. You need a way to plan and set goals that reflects that individuality. *Big Plan for the Creative Mind* seeks to offer this to you.

This book is an opportunity for the creative industry to get a glimpse of what it's like both in people's businesses and in their lives. As we were thinking through goal setting on a macro level, we wanted to represent a cross-section of industries and thought processes. The leaders included feature a variety of thought leaders on goal setting with all different approaches, and their profiles help you to understand why that style of goal setting works for them. We chose to interview the experts that create some of these tools we've mentioned. We wanted to spotlight their thinking and best practice advice in one place.

Inside each leader's profile, you will find:

- *Their MBTI, so you can get a glimpse at how their brain works.*
- *Their thoughts on goal setting.*

- *A brief lifestyle profile, so you can see what their day to day looks like.*
- *Why they choose to plan.*

By reading through each of the profiles, our hope is that you'll be able to pull pieces from each that can add up to the best customized goal setting solution for you. The end of the book includes a section in which we encourage you to write, reflect on your takeaways from the book, and start creating your own plan!

We want to connect with you. Tag us or connect with us on Instagram: @dannielynnfountain and @reinaandcompany and the hashtag #bpcmbook

Find more information at www.bpcmbook.com.

Let's get started!

INTRODUCTION

Meet the Authors

Authors

We can't wait to connect with you!
Use the instagram handles below and the hashtag #bpcmbook

Dannie Fountain
danniefountain.com
@dannielynnfountain
ENFJ

Reina Pomeroy
Reina + Co
Life + Biz Success Coaching®, Reina + Co
Creative Empire Podcast Host
@reinaandcompany
@mycreativeempire
ENTJ/ENFJ

Contributors

Lara Casey
Cultivate What Matters
@Lara Casey
@Cultivate What Matters
INFP

Lisa Jacobs
Your Best Year
@Iamlisajacobs
INTJ

Amber McCue
Business Operations Expert and Modern CEO Podcast Host
@ambermccue
ENTJ

Tara Newman
Leadership and Business Coach
@thetaranewman
INFJ

Jillian Smith
One Touch Events
@onetoucheventsllc
ESFJ - A

Lacey Sites
A Lit up Life
@alituplife
INTJ

Ashley and Graham Scobey
The Scobeys
@thescobeys
Graham - INFP
Ashley - ESTJ

INTRODUCTION

Jenna Kutcher
Photographer, Educator, Artist
@jennakutcher
ESFP

Natalie Franke
The Rising Tide Society & Honeybook
@nataliefranke
INFP

Courtney Johnston
Rule Breaker's Club
@courtbourtinc
ENFJ

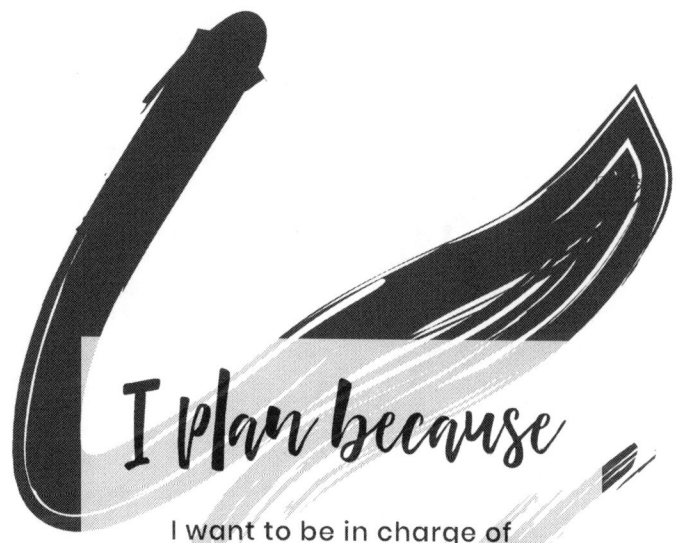

I plan because

I want to be in charge of creating the world around me.

– TARA GENTILE

NAME: *Tara Gentile*

MBTI PROFILE: **INTP**

Reverse-Engineering

Tara Gentile doesn't like to plan. She goes with the flow, decides her day when she wakes up in the morning, and sometimes lets herself wake up without an alarm. Yet, she's an awesome goal setter. So, what's her secret?

For Tara it's all about reverse-engineering. "I think people go really wrong when they try and figure out how to make it happen first, in order to set the goal," she says.

First of all, you need to decide where you want to be heading in a year from now. Then you start from the end point and work your way backward, breaking the goal into more manageable chunks. When you set the goal first, it gives you the "container" (as Tara calls it) that helps you figure out what it is you need to learn, what systems you need to put in place, and what people you need to bring in.

Setting Time Lines

Where do you want to be 12 months from now? Once you know the end goal and have broken it down into smaller chunks, you can assign time lines for each one and by when you want to achieve them. However, Tara says they need to remain flexible. If they're not, it can be tough to stick precisely to them.

How far out can you see? For most people it's about three months—maybe six. It's easier to set specific tasks for this part of your year-long goal and be able to stick to them. Tara suggests leaving the last quarter or two free a little more "up in the air"—to be determined by how well you accomplished the earlier tasks.

You can absolutely set tasks for the entire year; just remember that they can be flexible.

Keeping Focus

As someone who is more of a free spirit, Tara is constantly reminding herself to stay focused. It is good to remind yourself why you are excited, what you are working toward, and why it is important.

Keeping the main goal in the back of your mind will help remind you also why you're completing these tasks along the way.

"If I'm sending out emails or working in Asana, I'm doing it for the right reasons. I'm doing it for this one particular reason—this one goal that I have," states Tara.

When you don't keep your focus, it can be easy for your mind to drift away from your purpose. You can start thinking, "I don't want to do this" or "I'd rather be doing something else"—two thoughts that are not helpful at all. For Tara, it's focus first and then prioritization after that.

The Time of Year

There are a couple times in the year when Tara is the most focused. It's usually in January, around the beginning of the year (or sometimes the end of the prior year, in December). The next check-in point for setting goals is August or September.

Tara says right after summer is when she's re-energized and inspired by life, so it's a great time to recalibrate where she is, where the plan is, and what she needs to put into place for the remainder of the year.

Be willing to look out as far as possible at the beginning of the year, but also be willing to come back and ask:

- *Where am I in terms of my end goal?*
- *Where have I gone wrong?*
- *What do I want to do next?*
- *How can I use what I have to get to where I ultimately wanted to be?*

Planes or Plans?

Setting your goals doesn't always have to take place while sitting at your desk with all your supplies around you. It can take place anywhere at all. Tara happens to do most of her planning on planes. She travels a lot, so that's where she can usually fit it in.

"It's one of those spaces where you put the headphones on, you're in your little hole in your particular tiny, little space in the airplane. Someone's bringing you bubbly water on a regular basis, and you just sit down and it starts flowing," explains Tara.

Assessing Your Progress

It's important to remember not to get down on yourself if you don't happen to make your goal. Maybe you haven't judged the scenario properly or you've set unrealistic metrics. There are plenty of reasons why goals aren't achieved.

Tara says one of the saddest things is when people tell her, "Well, I've never met a goal. How can I set a new one?" Of course you can! There's no reason why you can't set a new goal. It's just about changing your approach.

After you've set a new metric, ask yourself:

- *What are my behavioral changes?*
- *What are all the structural changes I need to make?*
- *What are the mindset changes I need to make?*

Using metrics to define your success in terms of your goals can be extremely useful. According to Tara, a self-described "numbers person," it's easier to visualize it that way.

"I constantly have my eye on the numbers. Whether they're cash numbers, membership numbers, list numbers—whatever it might be, I've got my eye on that. It's never a surprise to me," she says.

Organizing Your Goals

There's never a question of which goals take priority for Tara: They're all under the umbrella of the main goal. Then come the quarterly goals, which are the chunks that were broken off the main goal earlier in the year.

It's helpful to think of your goals as a puzzle and figure out which pieces need to fit together in order for the whole picture to become clear. This way, nothing is vying for your sole attention. Instead, they're all just projects that have to get done and worked on. "Everything is very hierarchical for me, in that way, and it keeps me very, very focused," she says.

For example, Tara was recently faced with a challenge at work to get their subscriber numbers up to 1,000 people in 12 weeks. Once the goal was set, she had the task of breaking it down into projects. Think about it this way: What are the things that I need to do to make these projects a reality?

One thing was rebranding the website. Another was restructuring the team and hiring or promoting current employees. Both of these things count as projects that are working toward your goal.

Unfortunately, they didn't meet the goal, but they still achieved amazing results and high engagement. Every step you take toward achieving your end goal is helping to achieve it.

Not Meeting Your Goals

Not meeting a goal isn't something that Tara makes a big

deal out of. For her it's very much "a non-issue"—because life happens, right? She doesn't feel the need to give herself a pity party or wallow in disappointment or take the day off. What she does focus on, however, is self-care.

"If I don't hit my goals and I'm disappointed about it, it's probably because I haven't taken care of myself and I've let things stress me out. I've let things overwhelm me," she explains.

Canceling a few plans and letting yourself recharge after not meeting your goals will help you get back on track—refreshed and ready to go! It'll get you back into the mindset to readjust your goals.

Recently, Tara started using a paper planner to help organize her goals (Danielle Laporte's Daily Desire Map Planner, to be exact). It's useful to be able to visually map out where your free time is and what blocks of time you have to get projects completed. And if you don't meet a goal today, it's no big deal: just move it over to the next free block of time.

Staying on Track

It can seem like a cliché, but the thing that helps Tara get her focus back after finding herself falling off course is to just take a walk. "If my head is too full, if my life is too full, if things are feeling off, taking a walk generally fixes the vast majority of it," she explains.

If life is feeling "off" on a bigger scale, Tara tries to spend an entire weekend doing things just for her. You need to let the pressure off yourself and give yourself time to recover your thoughts and drive. Then you can tackle it again.

Goal Setting Advice

Don't strictly base your goal setting on past goals, especially if you haven't accomplished your previous ones. It won't lead to motivating behavior or changed outlooks if you're just sticking to what you know and have done.

For Tara, the whole point of goal setting is to "do something different to acquire something new." Another piece of advice she shares is basing your goals off what you know you can accomplish instead of attempting to accomplish something that's vastly out of reach. This will make them more achievable and easier to follow.

Tara's Planning Materials

Planning doesn't have to be a structured event. You don't need a bunch of fancy tools to help you set goals. For Tara, all she needs are her gel pens and a 5 x 7 Moleskin notebook (preferably gridded, although they're getting harder to find). Oh, and definitely some bubbly water to sip on.

I prefer a lot of flexibility. So, that involves not a lot of long-term planning. On a day-to-day basis it looks like a lot of hedonism. I do what I want to do. I'm not very disciplined in the traditional sense. Although, I think I have discipline in other ways. But it's not like I'm making myself a list of chores or tasks. It's more like, when I wake up I decide what I want to do. Do I feel like going for a hike? Or going to the museum? Or driving for hours in one direction to go see this thing, spur of the moment? There's lots of flexibility, spontaneity with a healthy dose of ambition.

I'm not generally the kind of person who's just going to be satisfied lying around, although I do a fair amount of that. When I'm really happy, when I'm really into it lifestyle-wise, it's this mix of flexibility with really a go-getter attitude about it.

I live in Lancaster County, Pennsylvania, home to the original American Amish population. So we have horse and buggies drive by our house every day, like once an hour. This is not an unusual phenomenon.

I am partnered, if that's a thing. We generally refer to each other as husband and wife, but we're not actually married. His name is Sean, and I have a daughter named Lola who lives with her dad, so part of the flexibility in our lifestyle is we're really a two-adult household the vast majority of the time that also gets the pleasure of having an eight-year-old around every so often, which is a lot of fun. We're big eaters, big beer drinkers, and big wine people. We love the good life, and so that tends to be what we spend our free time doing.

Favorite Season

It's always a toss-up between spring and fall. This is the time of the year I am operating on all cylinders. If I had to pick one, I would say fall.

Hidden Talent

I studied music in college, and trombone was my major for a long time. I was a double major in religion and trombone.

Food Philosophy

If it tastes good, you eat it. That's my food philosophy. I would probably have to think a little bit more about that, but the brighter the flavors, the better. Healthy food can taste good, too, but mostly if it tastes really good, you should eat it. That means, especially since meeting my partner, Sean, I have been exposed to a lot more. He's a much more adventurous eater. I'm willing to try a lot of different things, but he goes out of his way to be adventurous. Anyhow, I've tried a whole lot of different things that I would never have thought I would try in the last four or five years!

Tara Gentile is the founder of CoCommercial, a digital small business community for entrepreneurs serious about making money, impacting their communities, and transforming the lives of those they love. She's also the host of Profit. Power. Pursuit., a podcast that takes you behind the scenes of successful small businesses. *Entrepreneur* named it one of 24 top women-hosted podcasts for business owners.

She's the creator of Quiet Power Strategy®, a business design system that helps you break through the inevitable earning plateau, and a bestselling Money & Life instructor on CreativeLive. Tara's work has been featured in *Fast Company*, *Inc*, *DailyWorth*, *Forbes*, and *The Huffington Post*.

I plan because

I believe my actions today will enable me to be a part of a larger ecosystem that is driving us toward the betterment of humanity but especially for women.

— NATALIE FRANKE

NAME: __Natalie Franke__

MBTI PROFILE: __INFP__

Think About the Big Picture

When you think about goal setting, do you think about the "now" or do you think about years down the road? For Natalie Franke, looking at the big picture is a helpful part of setting goals. Her approach comes from her personality strengths, which "futurism" is a big part of.

"I'm thinking so far into the future, that [sometimes] it's not even in my lifetime, which is both a gift and a curse," she says.

Something Natalie asks herself is whether the goals she's working on are helping her to get to where she wants to be when she's "old, wrinkly," and 70 years old. Is that weird? No. It's helping her to see the big picture of her life and align her goals accordingly.

When you're using a futuristic approach to goal setting, it can be helpful to ask yourself:

- *Where is this goal going to take me?*
- *If I achieve this goal, where will it be driving me to?*
- *Is it taking me toward where I want to be?*

Think about whether or not this goal is going to affect you in your 20s, 30s, 40s, and so on. It can sound a bit scary at first but it's a great way to get a truly personalized grasp on your goals.

Is your goal something that your future children will be proud of you for? This is a meaningful question for Natalie. You can even go further than this if you're willing. For example, Natalie offers that a lot of us might not know what our great-grandparents did in day-to-day life—or even further back, to their parents. Are the goals we set today going to help us make an impact?

The choices we make today will affect our families 100 years from now. If you step up and speak out on an issue, will it help to pave a way for younger generations and little girls to do the same? These are just a few of the things Natalie thinks about when she's setting her short-term, long-term, and forever goals.

Breaking Down Goals

For Natalie, goal setting happens quite frequently. She likes to set goals annually as well as monthly. For example, this year she wants to write a book. It's a big goal. However, it becomes much more easily achievable when you break it down into monthly, weekly, and daily tasks.

Just because you're looking at goals as a big picture, that doesn't mean your steps to get there have to be massive as well. "Sometimes I'll literally have a to-do list with checks that are as simple as 'Email this person'. That's a task, not necessarily a goal, but it leads into the goal for the month," says Natalie.

Occasionally, Natalie will even find herself setting more emotion-based daily goals, like "choosing joy," or allowing herself lenience after making a mistake. It's different than her usual goal setting, something she describes as "kindness building" and helping her self-esteem.

Setting Goals with Intention

A helpful way to set goals is to look at your strengths and work off of those, like Natalie does, with being able to look at the big picture. Another strength she utilizes when goal setting is strategy. However, she warns against basing your goals strictly on strategy: "It's the double-edged sword," states Natalie.

One of her personal struggles is being *too* strategic at times—which can lead to goals not being authentically what she wants to accomplish. Setting your goals according to your true intentions, while incorporating strategy, is a terrific way to combat those struggles.

Using Specific Goal Times

Setting aside specific times in the year for goal setting is a surefire way to help you stay on track. Natalie usually reserves the five days post-Christmas to start on her annual goals. Admittedly, this year was a bit different because she was in the middle of a move, but that shouldn't deter a dedicated goal setter!

The goal setting process takes place in stages.

Stage 1: Reflection

Whether you're setting professional or personal goals, reflection is always a crucial step. What did you accomplish? What did you not? How are you feeling in your life right now? Jot things down so you can visually see what you need to improve on.

Stage 2: Forward Thinking

Now that you've got a brand new slate, it's already time to start thinking about when this year is over and you're back in this same stage next year, five days from Christmas. What do you want to be reviewing next year?

Stage 3: Creating Noise

Now is the time to begin preparing your goals for the year. You need to be focused and you need to have a clear of idea of where you want to go. For Natalie, putting on music helps her create white noise and get down to business. (Fun fact: She loves a Spotify playlist called Brain Food.)

Assessing Your Progress

Some of your goals will have simple outcomes to determine. For example, with Natalie's goal of writing a book, either you've written a book or you haven't. There's not really a gray area. Some goals are more complicated, though. Natalie confesses this might be a bit corporate, but she likes to measure success according to metrics. "The ability to measure something is actually important to me, even though I'm a creative," she says.

Early on in the goal setting process, it helps to determine what your measurements of success are going to be. That way when you come back around to the end of the year, you can easily say, "Yes, I completed my goal" or "No, I didn't" and figure out from there what steps could have been taken.

Choose a point halfway through the year to check back in on your goals as well. Sometimes when you revisit a metric you set in December, you realize it's *way* off and pretty unachievable. Natalie uses this time to tweak her initial goals so that they're more accomplishable for the end of the year.

However, don't just intentionally set goals lower to begin with! That would be missing the whole point, especially for Natalie, who's quite the dreamer.

"Normally I'm like, *Go for the moon!*" she says. "And then I'm like, *Well, I kind of need a rocket ship first. And so it's June and I'm still building the rocket ship.*"

The Positive Feedback Loop

As a self-described "feeler" and "sensitive soul," it can be easy for Natalie to get down on herself for not achieving her goals. What she had to learn early on was to celebrate her little wins along the way. You create a "feedback loop" in your brain that essentially repeats "I'm doing this" over and over as a kind of positive affirmation that you are following in the right steps.

You'll start to see the impact—guaranteed. Take people who are trying to lose weight, for example. It can seem like a negative, daunting task at first. Then, when you start to see a few results—no matter how small—it all seems worth it. It encourages you to keep moving forward. You start to almost amplify your efforts because you've turned something negative into something positive.

This kind of positive feedback can be applied to any kind of goal setting. Changing your mentality from "I'm never going to make it" to "Yes, I can do this" will have huge results on the outcome of your goals.

Shoot for the Moon

Year to year, goals can be exceptionally different. A few things that they should all have in common, however, are your drive, ambition, and readiness to take them on. In other words, you're shooting for the moon. Still, even with your focus and concentration, it's hard to divide your attention between too many goals.

This year, Natalie decided to try working on one hefty goal and approximately three smaller ones. Doing one thing really well is better than putting only half of the work into completing too many.

Natalie's ratio of goals has shifted to a more personal approach as she's reached the latter half of her 20s, and she thinks it might get higher as she gets older. Her goals generally revolve around a continuation of what she's already doing or to try something completely new.

Holding Yourself Accountable

Holding yourself accountable and knowing that you have the power to commit to your goals is essential in completing them. Natalie holds herself accountable by making sure that she's checking in on her goals and setting aside time to review and revisit them. Whether it's every month or every year, she knows she's the one who needs to make this happen for her life.

Set aside a day, whether it's Sunday or Wednesday, to check in on our goals and visualize them coming to life. Natalie relates it to your hair: You don't notice it growing every day but after six months you look back and see the progress. The same can be said for goals.

This all comes full circle to the positive feedback loops, too. When you've seen the progress you've made in whatever amount of time, you can start to praise yourself for it—or, in some cases, figure out what it is you need to change.

It's about pushing yourself. "You really have to, you know, stop eating donuts every day because you want to fit into your size-eight shorts. Like, come on, girl! You can do it!" she says.

However, holding yourself accountable isn't always an easy feat. Some people might need a friend or a life coach to keep them on the right track—and that's okay, too.

Life Gets in the Way

Things are always going to pop up unexpectedly in life. You don't have control over this. What you *can* control is how you react and the ways you counteract it. For Natalie, it comes down to quality over quantity. Sure, she may not have as much time to work on her goals as she'd like, but the time she does have she uses wisely and efficiently.

She allows life to purposely get in the way. "I have learned that being too rigid with myself and being too uptight about micro-managing every hour is not healthy both for me and the people around me," she states.

It's okay to let things slide, but just remember what still needs to get done and make it a priority to get back on track.

The Importance of Notebooking

Natalie has spiral-bound notebooks all over. "I will just get in there and what I'll do is kind of go back to my outline—I'm very bulleted—like, what were the messy doodles all over the page and what am I thinking and what am I feeling? So, I dive into a notebook and I kind of write everything down to process (it helps me process) and then get it on paper. I feel like once I've written something down—and everyone's different—but once I've written something down on that page, there's a truth to it, there's a realness to it. When we talk about accountability, it goes hand in hand. Right? If it's only in your mind, you can convince yourself that *Ah, I didn't really set that goal* but when you write it down, it is written there, which means you have a benchmark to really go back to."

What Happens When You Don't Meet a Goal

It can be tough when you don't meet your goals. But hey, it happens to the best of us, right? Instead of shutting down and getting upset over it, Natalie suggests asking yourself a few questions.

- *What did I not do right?*
- *How did I not make this goal?*
- *How did I not accomplish it?*

Ask yourself these questions first and foremost, but also ask the people around you whom you love and trust. It can be helpful to get an outside opinion in case you missed something that might seem like no big deal to you, but can be helpful for others. Or sometimes just hearing advice you already know out loud from someone you trust can be almost like a revelation.

Natalie says that after she's missed a goal, she allows herself time to mourn and be disappointed. Give yourself that room before moving onto the solutions. Then you can extend the time frame or rework the ideas behind your goal. No matter what, don't give up. There's always a solution right around the corner even if it's not clear to you right then and there.

lifestyle profile

I live in San Francisco, California. I'm a new transplant to the West Coast. I grew up and spent the majority of my life in Annapolis but all of my life on the East Coast. I moved out here with my awesome husband (who's my high school sweetheart) and our two dogs. Hunter, the rescue pup, we love him. He's just a big goober. And then Sophie, the miniature Australian shepherd, she's just a slight menace with a dash of adorableness. She's like a dog too smart for her own good and knows it, and knows she can get away with anything.

I am in a season of my life where we don't have children, we're not newlyweds anymore, but we really have two big focuses. One of them is the professional development for both of us. So we're really committed to the work we're doing. Notice how I said "the work we're doing" and not "work"? Because I think we're really committed to the impact we're making and trying to be intentional about where those hours go, because we don't have kids to invest that time in just quite yet, and we hope that comes one day.

The other thing is I think we're really committed to prioritizing quality time over the quantity of time, because we don't have a ton of it in this season. So, I just want to mention that because I think that's something that's really shaped everything from goal setting to just how I live my life in the day to day.

Your Most Repeated Intention

"Abundance" and "Gratitude"

What's Your Food Philosophy?

Carbs are life. Give yourself grace. Food that makes you happy, food that fuels your mind and body, and I think that changes from week to week, month to month, depending on our lives.

Most Admired Character Trait

I really admire selflessness in other people. I really believe that with human beings it's not something that necessarily comes naturally. Survival instinct is obviously very self-focused: Must survive, must procreate, must succeed. That's very reptilian brain, right?

So it's very rooted in humanity. However, I think higher-level consciousness and our social evolution have enabled selflessness a lot, especially in the female brain, just within humanity. So, when I see someone that has really channeled that well, like my hero, Mother Teresa. She was my hero growing up. I dressed up as her for Halloween. I was that weird kid.

bio

Natalie Franke is a photographer, educator, community builder, and one of the Founders of the Rising Tide. A graduate of the University of Pennsylvania, she studied visual studies with a focus on visual neuroscience and the psychology of seeing. Left brain meets right, she's a science nerd running on equal parts coffee and entrepreneurship.

Natalie currently lives in San Francisco with her husband and serves as the head of community for Rising Tide—leading a team of world changers in the pursuit of empowering the creative economy.

I plan because it gives me freedom.

— LACEY SITES

NAME: Lacey Sites

MBTI PROFILE: INTJ

Setting goals with intention shouldn't have to feel like a fight. Lacey Sites sets all her goals with intention, and says the process should feel like cultivation and creation. As founder of Lit Up Life, Lacey is committed to helping women escape the life they don't desire and build fulfilling, impactful businesses they truly want to run.

While focusing on intention in her business, Lacey also doesn't focus on the uncontrollable. A vague goal can be 1,000 followers, but actionable daily goals should look like outreach and opt-ins. The number is a consequence of the actionable goals.

Often, Lacey says, people fall prey to the arbitrary goal setting regime where they set goals around the outcomes of actions, rather than on the actions and the intentions themselves. She'll be specific about her results if she needs to be—for example, if she needs four clients to fill her practice—but she tries to be as unspecific in most other regards. If the number's 1,000, so what if she hits just below the mark, or way above? **As long as she's done her part and completed the steps necessary to get there, she's cultivated and created what she wanted.**

"What I've noticed in myself and basically all my clients is: **Where our focus goes, results show up**," Lacey says. "Every time, no matter what."

If she doesn't have a focus on something, she says it's "infinitely harder to create results." If she has a focus on too many things, the same applies. Intentions for Lacey are about where she's investing her attention. She trusts in the knowledge that results will come where they are meant to as a result of her work.

What Feels Good?

Lacey isn't the type to be motivated by pressure. Plenty are, but for Lacey and other INTJs, pressure can make goals harder to reach and worlds less enjoyable. "I also really love feeling like I don't have to do anything," she says. **"When the intention feels good and it doesn't feel like I *have to* but I *get to*, that's when I thrive."**

Lacey emphasizes that whatever you're doing—whether that's running a business or going to school—it should feel good. "If you're setting goals that make you feel really icky all the time, or make you feel less than, or make you feel like you're never going to make them, that's a problem."

She says a "goal win" should feel like a stretch, but a good one. Goals that are too big—especially ones set without the right intentions—can cause little more than anxiety and the strong inclination to give up. When you feel good about the a goal you're setting and know the steps are within your power, the goal itself feels good.

Too many intentions or goals at once can also lead to disaster central. Lacey instead focuses on one at a time. As soon as she's finished devoting her time and energy to one goal, she evaluates what needs to be done elsewhere (or on the same path) and moves her focus there.

"Right now, I'm coming into a launch and I know 100% that's my intention. That's my focus," she says. "When I finish one, the next one begins."

It's a Never-Ending Series of Celebrations

Because Lacey's goals are more about intention than outcome, all her little victories get celebrated along the way, rather than just the product of her actions in total. Her journey is less a repeated "action and result, action and result" journey; hers is more of a seamless journey with overall assessments.

Lacey compares entrepreneurship to a never-ending train. "It's not like, 'Get the thing. Action. Result. Action. Result.'" She says it's more like:

- *Overall, am I increasing my income?*
- *Am I increasing my list size?*
- *Am I feeling good most of the time?*
- *Am I building a team in a way that feels good?*

If all of the above are happening, particularity doesn't mean a thing.

Meshing Flow with Accountability

In Lacey's old job, she did a ton of fundraising, and that fundraising involved continuous, heavy goals. She was pushed by a deadline-driven schedule and realized the beauty of flexible, intentions-driven goal setting as an entrepreneur. She knew she could hit hard deadlines and focus on outcomes, but she didn't want to deal with the high—not to mention unnecessary—level of anxiety.

"**[My current system] lets me create really good results, but not at the expense of sleep or well-being,**" she says.

So, what does Lacey do when she's launching or working on projects with her team? She sets deadlines—but only for the small stuff. When she's working on projects with her team, she'll outline deadlines and time frames for specific steps, because these are things she and the people she works with can control. They're not faraway numbers. They're real, actionable steps that are done today, tomorrow, next week, and the week after that.

She leaves the results—such as the numbers of people who take part in her programs, the profits made, and more "uncontrollable" aspects—to the Universe.

The Triangle Exercise

To figure out what stuff she needs to cover and what stuff is out of her hands (Universe stuff), Lacey uses the Triangle Exercise. Basically, she puts her goal at the top and divides it into two different corners: the stuff she controls and the stuff she doesn't.

Everything on her side are the things she loves to cover and will gladly structure with deadlines, time frames, and clear steps. Everything on the other side, she loves to be "flow-based" about. She shows up for her side, does her deeds, and lets the results on the other side be what they may be.

The "Universe side" generally consists of things like:

- *Bringing in the right clientele for a service.*
- *Showing the right audience a certain opportunity.*
- *Gaining X number of program members, clients, etc. in a given time frame.*

The things that the Universe controls are the things Lacey has been teaching herself to let go of for years. As a recovering control freak, she says it's important for her to identify those.

"[On the other side] is stuff that I know I have to physically show up and take action around," Lacey says. These are the steps and mini-goals she accomplishes.

For the "control" corner of her triangle, Lacey uses several tools to help track her movements and set her deadlines. Basecamp and Google Docs are valuable resources for launching time, while Satori, Google Calendar, and a trusty Day Designer are used to manage and schedule her life, in and outside of finances and clients.

Coping with Not Meeting Intentions

Sometimes, things happen. Maybe you don't pull your

weight on your side of the triangle, or life gets in the way. Lacey doesn't let missed goals get her down for long. She's confident enough as an entrepreneur to know that these things happen—that business goes on—and she sets sail for success again.

"I really don't expect this entrepreneurial journey to just look really good all the time," she says. "I really believe that it's fine and it's for my benefit in some way, shape, or form." Lacey grew up in a family of successful entrepreneurs and is grateful to have had the inside scoop from a young age.

"For me, if something doesn't happen, I need to look at my side of the triangle and see what I didn't do well," she says. Keeping on keeping on is in her nature. She adds, "If something was wrong, I'd probably spend a total of 10 minutes thinking about it and I'd just move on."

She acknowledges that moving on so quickly is a trained skill. Many are prone to wallowing in their losses and struggles, and it takes practice and diligence to "train your brain," as Lacey puts it. When in grad school, she was a perfectionist and recalls times when she was entirely consumed by a grade less than a 4.0. Eventually, she was forced to realize she could no longer live with such a perfectionist and controlling mindset.

"I literally decided one day, 'I can't let stuff like this control me anymore, so my job is not to control these things. My job is to start controlling my brain.'"

Since then, Lacey has been focused on reworking her thoughts, reprogramming her subconscious mind, and showing up differently to her own work.

Tools for Mindset Reprogramming

To get to her zen, out-of-my-control mindset, Lacey has found solace in the book *A Course of Miracles* by Helen Schucman, the stop sign method, regular meditation and tapping.

She says that while the stop sign method might seem simple, it's infinitely helpful. Whenever a thought that does not serve her enters her mind, she pictures a stop sign and holds it there until she knows she will not let herself go any further. The stop sign method serves as both an immediate distraction and a way to train your brain. Lacey compares it to Pavlov's dog—to an extent.

The stop sign is especially helpful because it prevents argument with a thought, working through the logic and convincing yourself you're right each and every time. "What I've noticed is when I don't engage in [the thought] is actually when I feel less stressed," Lacey says.

Tapping, also called Emotional Freedom Technique or EFT for short, also helps Lacey reduce her anxiety. If she's feeling the need for control or perfectionism, tapping puts a damper on her anxiety. It can be practiced by taking a negative emotion, memory, fear, or anxiety, and tapping with your fingertips several times on each of the body's meridian points. "If I'm in an anxious place, tapping helps a lot," Lacey said. "It's not a daily practice. It's more like an in-the-moment tool."

While tapping, she will sometimes say out loud the problem on her mind, and she finds that this helps bring to light its insignificance.

Managing Personal and Business

Unlike many others who will neglect to care for themselves during particularly busy business times, Lacey has an autoimmune disease and can't go without self-care. She says the negative consequences of a lack of self-care are, in a way, a gift because they force her to take care of herself.

Regardless of whether you need self-care to physically function each day, Lacey says it's key to the best success. "I've seen this in people I've worked with. When we come to coaching, business, *et cetera* from a full cup, success happens." When Lacey approaches business from an empty cup, on the other hand, it can be difficult to fulfill her clients' business needs.

When you can't do it for yourself, you can't do it for others. Or, you can—but it'll be a poor experience, Lacey says.

In the early stages of her business, Lacey was under the impression that planning might take away her freedom. Now, she says, she realizes that planning provides more space and more freedom, not less.

"Ultimately, planning feels like a gift to myself," she says.

lifestyle profile

I used to be super strict about this. I had to look a certain way and now I just give myself anywhere between 30 and 45 minutes, and I just do what I feel like I need. So, I have to check in with myself first. Like, "What do I need right now?" Sometimes I need to journal and get all the crap out of my head, or sometimes I need to tap, or meditate, or whatever, but it basically involves doing something for me.

Secret Talent

I'm like an animal whisperer. I worked at a vet all through college and if there was ever a mean dog or one that wouldn't behave, that was always my gig. I find animals all the time that are lost or whatever. It's just a thing. I'm an animal whisperer. It's totally my hidden gift.

Reading Recommendation

My favorite book ever, *The Magic of Believing*. It's such an old book. It was written in the 1940s. The author is Claude Bristol and I just love it and I listen to it probably three times a year.

bio

Lacey Sites is a business mentor and success coach for high-performing women entrepreneurs. She has her MS in mental health counseling and her MBA She's been a therapist, the director of a $45 million/year non-profit, and is the proud owner of two successful online businesses. She's the founder of A Lit Up Partnership, and was also the co-host of the Leading Greatly Podcast. It's her mission to help other women build and grow their own service-based business that truly lights them up, and gives them the personal and financial freedom and impact.

I plan because

the alternative is to use the gift of this life by accident.

— LARA CASEY

NAME: **Lara Casey**

MBTI PROFILE: **INFP**

Setting Heart Goals

When you imagine goal setting, you might imagine that you have nothing in common with Lara Casey. She says she does things quite differently than most of the world and we'd have to agree. You might envision a hyper-motivated, ultra-organized productivity machine, and while she's motivated, she'd argue that it's not an innate skill and that it didn't come naturally to her in the beginning. Traditional goal setting gives her the "heebie jeebies" because it is pressure filled and is focused on quick outcomes. And while it focuses on getting you to the finish line, you miss the heart and intention in between, which Lara argues is the most valuable part.

Lara doesn't ascribe to the pressure-filled goal setting model, and she has found a way to uncover people's "good goals" and helping people achieve them. Good goals are about cultivating what you've been given: your relationships, your time, your money, your possessions, your work, your children, your home. It's not about creating a goal out of thin air that sounds good and is going to make you do more, it's about using what you do have already and using it well.

In Lara's former life as a personal trainer, a lot of clients would come to her with a number. When a client would say something like "I want to lose 10 pounds," her response would be "Why 10 pounds?" It turns out it was just an arbitrary weight that he was in college, and there was no real heart connection behind that goal.

Digging in deeper to the deeper meaning of *why* it was important to him in the big picture, he said "I want to be fit and healthy so that I can live long enough to walk my daughter down the aisle." Those *heart reasons* are the things that keep us motivated and keep us doing the hard things.

When a goal or a number like 10 pounds is connected to something that's going to make you want to get up out of bed every day and put your feet on the floor and get to it, no matter how many times you fall down, that's when you know you have a good goal. That's the key. That type of goal allows you the freedom and grace to step into little by little progress and to imperfect progress. It's not about making perfect progress. It's about just being on the right path.

Examine Your Life

The process starts 20 steps before you even set goals. You have to first evaluate what worked and what didn't work, over the last calendar year or whatever period you choose. You have to first look back before you can start to look at what's next. Most of us just want to move forward when we're setting goals, but the past has a lot to teach us in terms of where to focus in the future.

An exercise that helps to evaluate the different areas of life is the wheel of life. It is an exercise that allows you to evaluate your satisfaction in different areas of your life: personal relationships, work, finances, family, faith.

Instead of just looking at the narrow focus (people usually do a year, or the circumstances that are in front of them), **look at what you want life to look like when you're 80 years old**. That question creates an immediate mental shift for people, because it makes you ask yourself, "If that's where I want to be when I'm 80, then why am I doing what I'm doing today? What am I doing about that today?"

As far as a number goes, this is also a place where people get hung up with goal setting. You might feel like there's some magic number that you're supposed to have. Last year, Lara had two goals. They were big picture, overarching things because she was in a season of change and of transition.

This year, Lara has boiled it down to four goals. Those four goals are big picture–focused and are broken down into monthly goals, weekly goals, and daily goals, with tasks and projects underneath those. Those four goals help to remember why she is doing them in the first place, because when we lose sight of why and what it's connected to, we start to set goals like the personal training client, striving toward a goal that is born out of guilt and not out of what matters.

Fresh Start: There's No Magic in January 1st

There's nothing special about January 1st. But, there is something about the forward momentum of a new calendar year. You can use the January 1st mark as a milestone to check in on the progress you have throughout the year, but you don't have to wait until a new year to start making progress toward your goals. Lara is constantly reevaluating goals by using PowerSheets, which has a goal check-in each quarter that helps evaluate the growing and shifting that happens in life and with the goals.

PowerSheets have a strong structure of checking in on progress. This year, they have what's called a progress bar, so there are monthly goals, weekly goals, and daily goals, and it's that mental check-in that allows you to measure your progress. That's something that traditional goal setting lacks as well: the ability to measure progress. It's all about checking off the giant check mark at the very end, but there's no focus on the in-between and the little by little. The little by little, the in-between, that progress—that's where life happens. That's the good stuff. The way you evaluate it is by checking in on it frequently.

Planning Doesn't Have to Be Perfect

One thing you don't need is the perfect pen or the perfect circumstances or the perfect amount of time or total silence. We have in our generation, especially as creative entrepreneurs, gotten stuck. With big bold letters.

S-T-U-C-K.

Because we think that we have to have it all together in order to even start considering setting goals. That's what you don't need. What you do need, then, is an attitude of focusing on making a mess, which means just digging in right where you are, even if your circumstances aren't perfect, and owning the fact that you don't have to have perfect words to write goals. Those are the mental things that you need.

Physically, it depends on your personality type. Lara is the type of person for whom writing words helps process thoughts. Other people may be more visual and add sketching or visual creation to help them to visualize where they want to go, so have the tools that fit your personality, not what Instagram says is nice.

In order to create an environment that's conducive to getting in the right frame of time to goal set, use the power of stepping away. As creative entrepreneurs, Lara notes that there's a tendency to have a narrow focus, and when the focus is too narrow on our tasks, our goals, our action steps, our strategy, we might need to step outside and take a deep breath and come back refreshed. When working on big projects like writing or taking action on goals, going outside has been helpful for Lara in getting more clarity.

Another tool that Lara uses to set herself up for

goal-crushing success is her calendar. She considers the calendar an underused power tool in getting things that matter done and to setting herself up for success in what matters. When you put something on your calendar, you're planting a seed, and it's important to plant seeds of rest and renewal and refreshment, as well as seeds of being able to plan for things. Make time for what matters. If you don't make time for it and have check-ins to remind yourself to do it, it's not going to grow.

You Can't Predict the Future

It's inevitable that things are not going to grow as you expect, because you can't predict the future. If you follow Lara on social media, you'll know that she's an avid gardener. When she grows tomatoes, she never knows which direction those vines are going to grow, the exact date when there will be fruit, how many pieces of fruit are going to come, what day they're going to bloom; it's exactly the same with planning and being intentional: We don't know the exact outcomes, but we have to prepare ahead of time in order for fruit to come at all. Lara's advice is to to keep tending, no matter what the outcome of that goal is going to be.

When life takes a turn or things grow, Lara tells us that is cause for celebration because it means that there's growth. A nonlinear path is something that society is unsure of because we like straight-lined plans. In generations past, there was an expectation that all follow an expected path. The younger generations are breaking that mold and charting their own courses.

There are times when goals won't get met. When you

don't meet a goal, redirect.

Lara suggests you stop and ask yourself three questions:

1. *Am I not motivated about this particular goal?*
2. *Have I lost sight of the why?*
3. *Am I just not connected to this goal? Is this actually not something that's important to me?*

If a *heart goal* is important enough, you'll do it. If it is not important, maybe you need to change the methods and change up the approach to the goal. When it's not working, it's important to stop to redirect and evaluate what's going on. Whatever you find, Lara says that you should **give yourself permission to change course and to change direction, with the possibility of changing the plan entirely**.

In the example of her garden, Lara says that you have to be ready to completely change course. The plants might grow to be 10 feet taller than expected, just as it might in life. We're all following paths that have not been chartered yet, so if you come up to a place in your life where goals didn't turn out the way you thought, or something didn't grow in the direction that you thought it would, celebrate: It means that something is growing. Stop and reevaluate how to support that growth.

Tough Love

What Lara sees is that people who aren't doing it "right" or have struggled with goal setting successfully get caught up in the system instead of actually doing the action steps. **People get caught up in planning, instead of actually**

planting the things that we should be planting to grow an intentional life. She encourages users of PowerSheets or any planning system to break the rules. You don't have to use PowerSheets or any other tool exactly how everybody else does; make sure that it works for you.

Lara strongly encourages people to give those systems a chance. Don't just give up the first time it doesn't work. She says, "If the Wright Brothers did that, they wouldn't have flown. They fell down many times over." You're like the Wright Brothers in the planning process. Make sure you're giving the system, the goal, or the process time to take root.

The problem isn't about the tools or the fact that the goals are necessarily bad. Lara argues that "**we are in a culture that lacks discipline.**" Since many of us can easily lose sight of where we should be putting our time based on what's truly important, we end up spending time and energy on things of low or no importance.

"How we spend our time is how we spend our lives," Lara states.

Learning discipline and asking for advice can be a way to kick-start success. The number-one heartache that Lara has for our culture is seeing people who so badly want to grow a meaningful business or an intentional life lack the discipline to achieve their dream. Some might believe that hard work isn't the answer, but in Lara's mind, there's no substitute for hard work.

We Don't Have to Do it All

There is a misconception that we must do it all and that we have to achieve and produce constantly. To use a gardening metaphor, what about enjoying the harvest and the fruits of your labor? Enjoying the season of rest doesn't imply never working again; it is meant to encourage taking rest in order to do better work that comes from a place of peace and rest. It's not difficult to imagine: You'd be better for your clients, your family, for yourself. You will be a more inspired creative all because the inspiration is coming from living life rather than staring at a computer screen.

Point Your Arrow

Lara says, "One thought that I feel like is important is something my friend Lysa TerKeurst said: that every decision we make has an arrow attached to it. These arrows point us in one direction or another. Your decision arrows, they have the power to either fly through distractions and all the lies. Maybe it's fear. Maybe it is feeling inadequate, or feeling ill equipped, or feeling like you're not an expert in your creative field, whatever it is. Or, maybe you feel too young or too old, imperfect—anything. They have the potential to cut through all of that and hit the target. Alternatively, the decisions that you make can flail around and float, because maybe you don't even know what the target is.

"I want my arrows aimed at the target, and my encouragement for you is that it is better to have your arrows aimed at a target that even feels a little unsure than to be aimed at no target at all. Goals don't have to be perfect or expertly executed or written—it is important to have a direction. You have to be the person to point that arrow. Being intentional is all about is about aiming your arrows intentionally in the right direction."

lifestyle profile

Source of Inspiration or Motivation

Somebody asked me recently, a couple weeks ago, how I have so much energy and motivation. You know, I try to eat healthy foods. I exercise, and I try to get rest, but what really motivates me is thinking about where I was and where I am now. I am so grateful. My life is worlds different from 10 years ago when I first started my first creed of business as a wedding planner. You know, sometimes I lose sight of that big picture, but nothing motivates me more than that. That's why I do what I do. I wake up every day, and think I am not in that dark, awful place anymore, and I want to help people to not feel like they have to be in that place, either.

What Does Your Morning Ritual Look Like?

For me, I have to say this. A friend of mine, Simon—I didn't want to say *Simon said to me,* because it sounds weird, but my friend Simon once told me that "how you start the day determines the day," and that has stuck with me ever since. What I do—and I should say this, too, is that this doesn't mean that you have to strive for perfect circumstances. I think people mistake that in goal setting, in creed of entrepreneurship, in life in general, is that we have to strive for perfect circumstances in a perfect structure. I have learned the opposite is true of that.

For me, my morning is about focusing the arrows of my heart and my time and my feet and my hands at life-giving inspiration. I read scripture first thing in the morning, even if it's just on my phone. I exercise in the morning with the kids, and it doesn't matter if the whole day is thrown off by crying babies or whatever, as long as I am on that path and have the attitude of grace and determination.

You know, I've had some pretty chaotic mornings, too. You just learn to roll with the punches.

Sunday Soundtrack?

My Sunday soundtrack is twofold. There's one melodic line of children squealing and screaming, which sounds terrifying, but it's beautiful. It is the most lovely music to hear my kids just playing out in the dirt or the garden or running around in diapers. Then, I love Gospel music. Nothing fires me up more. Those two things combined make for a real good Sunday.

bio

Lara Casey is a believer in the impossible, helping women to live on purpose through the many hats she wears in her parent company, Cultivating What Matters. Lara is passionate about helping people get unstuck, unrushed, and living on purpose instead of by accident. She created the PowerSheets™ grace-filled goal setting planner, the Write the Word™ journals, and founded Southern Weddings a decade ago. She's also the founder of the Making Things movement. She lives in Chapel Hill, North Carolina, with her husband, Ari, and their three children.

I plan because

dreams happen when
they're due.

— ASHLEY SCOBEY

I don't want to have regrets
at the end of my life.

— GRAHAM SCOBEY

NAMES: __Ashley + Graham Scobey__

ASHLEY MBTI PROFILE: **ESTJ**

GRAHAM MBTI PROFILE: **INFP**

If your business is leaving you burnt out, Ashley and Graham Scobey will tell you it's because you're not following your real passions. Your life shouldn't be your business; your business should reflect your life. It should include your values as a human being and what truly excites and inspires you, and it should curb that burnt-out feeling and leave you totally satisfied at the end of every day.

The Scobeys know all too well burnout syndrome, having started a business that didn't reflect their values back in 2008. Ashley and Graham were high school sweethearts with a love of photography. They turned their hobby into a photography business—shooting, Graham says, "a little bit of everything"—and quickly discovered that they were not fulfilled by their work. After six months, the couple hit their burnout point. They were forced to take a break and reassess.

Ashley and Graham considered their purpose as people:

- *What were their strongest beliefs?*
- *What did they want their life's work to be?*
- *What were their values?*
- *Who were they, as people?*

The couple used their answers to these questions as a foundation to build their new business upon—and that's when things took a satisfying turn.

They started photographing weddings, reflecting their convictions that:

- *People are good.*
- *Good relationships are the most incredible experiences people can have.*
- *Empathy, service, and sacrifice are essential.*
- *Moments are fleeting and should be celebrated and cherished.*

"We started working with couples—couples who'd just gotten engaged or couples who had been married for 10 years," Graham says. "Everything just kind of clicked."

The Scobeys waved *bye-bye* to burnout.

Grounding in Purpose

Ashley and Graham may be opposite MBTIs, but they've worked out a planning system. Following their common values, the Scobeys set goals with unwavering intention.

In their early days, Ashley says, they weren't so intentional about goal setting. She and Graham "just kind of looked around at what other people were doing," which was a direct path to dissatisfaction. If another photographer spoke at a conference, they felt they needed to speak at a conference. If another photographer won an award, they felt they needed to compete. They tried to match their income to others' income, but the couple found themselves driven off course and empty inside when they reached their "goals."

What the world tells you, Ashley says, is that you have to be heard over all the noise. You have to be "blown around" by the winds of your industry trends.

"We tried to be louder, and we tried to be bigger," Ashley says. "We tried all that." But this goal setting process was not fulfilling and had no purposeful direction. **Ashley and Graham weren't connecting their goals to who they were at their core.**

After reaching several empty goals on a lax time frame, Ashley says, "We realized that was not an effective way to set goals. It wasn't measurable and time-sensitive, and it also wasn't a fulfilling way to set goals. It didn't mean anything to us."

These days, Ashley and Graham use the *why* system for generating intentional goals, which means ensuring their goals are connected to their purpose. When they're able to follow through on those goals by making them measurable and time-sensitive, their purpose is fulfilled faster and with accuracy.

Instead of giving in to the temptation to get bigger and louder, and follow trends in your industry, Ashley recommends **getting smaller, getting quieter, and grounding yourself in who you are.**

Graham says, "You can have all the gifts and talent in the world, but if you don't know yourself, those things will go to waste. Those things aren't grounded in purpose—you're just stacking talents that can be blown over by the wind."

Taking the time for introspection is often what is needed to build a successful business. If you structure your business around your strong and unique abilities, you're setting yourself apart for success. Cultivating your authentic strengths will catapult you in ways *going with the flow* never will.

"What is the point of being in a creative industry if you don't use your unique gifts, your unique talents, your unique personality?" Ashley asks. She adds that you must be okay with the fact that your business and your life won't look like everyone else's. This fact is a gift, she says. A superpower.

The Practical Method

Graham and Ashley sit down together every now and then with pen and paper on hand to reassess their purpose and goals that will align with that purpose. They take personality tests to better understand their strengths, weaknesses, and tendencies. They look at goal setting holistically rather than through segments.

Holistic goal setting is important, Graham says. In the beginning, he and Ashley didn't practice holistic goal setting, which proved a recipe for disaster. Graham would, for example, spend a chunk of time one day working out at the gym to stay healthy and would spend the entire next day making up for lost work time on his computer. During this second day, he'd eat anything available and would leave no time for exercise. Both **staying healthy** and **maintaining business** were valuable and important goals to have, but they worked against each other when they weren't integrated.

"I thought I had to choose one or the other, and what happened was I chose neither," he says.

Ashley adds that goals should be integrated and should inform one another. When they aren't integrated, she warns, "they end up kind of cannibalizing each other."

The Four Ps of Productivity

The Scobeys follow a method called the "four Ps of productivity" when goal setting. Once a year, they take time out to have a long, introspective conversation on where they want to head together, which usually falls in their down season of January, February, and March. They hire a sitter for their children, or hunker down late at night to discuss the four Ps:

- *Personal*
- *People*
- *Play*
- *Priority*

The Scobeys write down all their long-term personal, people, and play goals, then head into prioritizing mode. This part, Ashley says, is the most difficult and rewarding.

"You can have it all; you can't have it all at the same time," she says. While filling out the four Ps exercise, it's important to remember that reaching prioritized goals will often help you reach other goals you've had to let go of. You'll have more time to pursue those goals later on, or your prioritized goals will create a positive side effect for those goals you had to put on the back burner.

Ashley and Graham set one-to-three-year prioritized goals, then break them down into manageable chunks—objectives they can revisit on a more frequent basis.

If their big goal, for instance, is to become international destination wedding photographers, they will break that goal down into periods, asking themselves:

- *What do we need to do in the next six months?*
- *Three months?*
- *This week?*
- *Today?*

The main goal remains the same, only aided by the implementation of short-term strategies and tactics. The breakdown of objectives goes into their calendar, a solidifying step that Ashley says is essential to their sense of accountability. "That makes it a tangible thing you can follow through on."

The Scobeys set accessible goals. They like to know exactly when they have reached those goals. In fact, they wouldn't actually set a goal like their example of "international destination wedding photographers"; they'd more likely set one with real measurements, such as "wedding photographers who shoot 10 weddings each year in international locations."

This way, they'll know exactly when they've reached their goal, and nothing is left open to interpretation. Graham adds that you could shoot one international wedding in your life or 20 per year and call yourself an international wedding photographer. Knowing that your goal is *10 per year* makes a big difference in tracking success.

Breaking down the 10-per-year goal into smaller measurements is the next step. To reach that goal, the Scobeys might reach out to their network the first month to see if they gain any interest, then reach out to three destination wedding planners the month after that, then proceed to create a "Five Things I Love About Destination Weddings" blog post. These are reasonable, timely steps moving them closer to their big dreams.

Keeping on Track

While the Scobeys believe environment is crucial to productive, uninterrupted goal setting time (heading out of the house or getting down to business at a quiet time of day), they also believe in the power of keeping reminders in their lives.

Ashley recommends putting goals in a visible place, like a calendar or a big sheet of paper. "Then put that on the wall so you have to look at it every single day," she says. Ashley also recommends putting reminders in your purse or setting your goals as your smartphone background.

"The more you can keep those things top of the mind, the more you can start to run your decision-making through them," Graham says. Any time you look at your steps, you'll have the opportunity to examine whether they're truly helping you move forward.

Drive Toward Your Goals—or Conduct a Science Experiment

Ashley and Graham chase their goals using car maneuvers and scientist experiments. Driving is a fluid process, just as pursuing goals is. When you're driving and see the car ahead put on their brakes, you can swerve around it or slow down.

The same goes with goals, Graham says. "If we start taking action today, we can figure it out: *Are my tactics working? Am I doing this well? Can I actually accomplish this in the time line that I put on it?*" If ever you arrive at a place where things aren't working out, you can reassess, rebuild, and rediscover how to accomplish that goal.

The "build-measure-learn" cycle ensures that you rarely experience failure. Because you're able to pivot to accommodate your goals, they remain possible. "[The cycle] redefines the idea of failure. It's not a matter of if; it's just a matter of when," Ashley says.

Ashley and Graham say this method is especially useful for artists, who often take failure personally and are prone to giving up. The "build-measure-learn" method is one scientists tend to use. They outline what they would like to better understand or learn more about, and if their experiment doesn't turn out the way they expected or hoped, they are simply grateful for having discovered all the wrong options.

It's a simple process of elimination that creatives can adopt for realistic goal setting and a healthier mindset.

As Thomas Edison said about his 10,000 attempts to create the lightbulb, **"I have not failed. I've just found ten thousand ways that don't work."**

Setting Business Goals Around Family Life

Ashley and Graham aren't ones to set hard objectives for their family life. They're more likely to set objectives for their business, and work that business around the things that matter most to them at home—like homeschooling their children. Shooting 40 to 50 weddings each year together would be an unrealistic goal for parents who homeschool. The couple will, though, shoot separately to accommodate consistent learning time with their daughter.

Ashley and Graham are still ironing things out in planning their home and business lives. But they say that the most important thing is to try to plan.

Living with No Regrets

Ashley and Graham agree that it's fine to not plan for some things, like the details of a vacation. They're familiar with the *get off the plane and* then *find a rental car and hotel* situation—and it's A-OK (if a little inefficient) to be that way.

However, the Scobeys agree that planning is paramount to living the life you truly want. Planning is the way to get your dreams out of the Bermuda Triangle of Time and move them into reality. Your dreams live in a quadrant of time, Ashley says, and if you don't make time to visit this quadrant, you'll never achieve them.

"This is our life we're talking about," Graham says. "This is the one shot we have. The thing that motivates us to plan out our goals is that there's a lot more weight to these things than there is to vacation, or to an adventure that's going to last a couple days." Life is short, Graham says. Every year that goes by goes faster, and it's important to ask yourself: *Will I regret not doing this when I'm 80?*

Will you regret not taking the time to be intentional about your life?

Ashley encourages those who aren't good at planning to write down their dream on a piece of paper. Write a letter to that dream, including what it will mean to you if you achieve it. Then, write what it will mean to you if you continue to put off that dream—to postpone it to another day or a better time. This, she says, will motivate you to create an action plan.

Ashley plans because dreams happen when they're due. For her, planning is the only means to an end of making the things that matter most to her happen.

Graham plans because he knows he has only one short life, and if he's not intentional with his time here on Earth, he will reach the end of his life and regret the way he lived.

Set your dream due date. Get planning.

lifestyle profile

Ashley: We have two kiddos, a two-and-a-half-year-old and a seven-year-old. We homeschool our seven-year-old, and I'm not currently worried about our two-and-a-half-year-old's education. He just gets what he gets! In our non-business life, we really love skiing and hiking. We live in Colorado, so the outdoors are our thing. We try to be very intentional about community building. So, investing in our friendships and our family relationships, and even business relationships in our geographical area and beyond.

Favorite Season

Graham: I love the fall for a lot of reasons. I feel like the weather's always gorgeous, and the scenery—I just love the leaves changing. I love the beauty that fall brings. I like the transition into the colder, too. I'm somewhat of a cold-weather person. I like to ski and do those kinds of things, so fall is a welcome relief. Especially because we just moved from Atlanta.

Ashley: My favorite season is spring, because outside of hanging with my kids and my hubby, gardening is my favorite thing in the entire world. I think there's something really special about being able to bring something out of dirt, and so spring is when I get to go through that process of deciding what plants I'm going to plant, and getting them all into the ground, and sharing that with our daughter, who has been my gardening helper!

Biggest Indulgence

Graham: I think experiences, for me. I try and go skiing once a week when the weather allows that, so I've been taking our daughter a lot. That's like her PE classes; we'll go up into the mountains and ski. That's kind of indulgent—spending a whole day doing something that's not work-related.

Ashley: You know what's interesting, though? I feel like indulgence is such a subjective thing. I think a lot of people would look at a lot of things that we do as a family and consider them indulgent, and we're like, those are non-negotiables for us. For example, getting out into the mountains and having time to just get into our own physical and mental health. Those things, I totally can see how that would be considered an indulgence, but for us it's not. Experiences, too. We don't ever turn down a chance to drive somewhere fun, or fly somewhere, and do adventurous things as a family.

bio

Ashley taught Graham that, when you really like someone, you intertwine your fingers. They've been holding hands that way ever since. Between then and now, they have dreamed their way from Los Angeles to Connecticut to Atlanta to Colorado. They've had the opportunity to work on

Oscar nominated films, they've had the privilege of building an internationally recognized photography studio, and they have been honored by being named one the 30 Rising Stars of Wedding Photography by *Rangefinder Magazine*. They have shot weddings and photojournalism and stupid big dreams, and work has received awards such as Junebug's Best of the Best, PDN Top Knots, and Showit's Image of the Year. More importantly, though, they are in constant search of ridiculous places to have dance parties and tickle fights with their two kids. Because, for them, their success will always be measured by the joy they exhibit and how well they love others.

I plan because it takes the crazy out of life and brings me massive freedom.

– AMBER MCCUE

NAME: **Amber McCue**

MBTI PROFILE: **ENTJ**

Setting Goals Is Easier than You Think

For Amber McCue, goal setting is a simple process. There's no need for it to be grand, she says. Just set one. It doesn't have to be elaborate, either. Research has shown that when you're setting goals, you're generally happier about your life. And who doesn't love a little extra happiness?

The idea of setting goals can seem intimidating at first. Or maybe seem a little too rigid, superficial, or restricting. But it doesn't have to be. After all, setting goals is all about you.

"Set a goal that fills your heart and has meaning for you," says Amber.

Once you set a goal, your subconscious begins to manifest those ideas—and there's huge power in that. The more times you subconsciously think of or see your goal, the more likely it is to be achieved. One of Amber's tips is to memorize your goals and also stick them on Post-its around your desk.

"While we're working, we're looking at that goal card," she says. "It's getting fried and burned into our subconscious."

From then on, we really just have to kick back and let the goal set in. Well, it's not quite that easy, but our subconscious minds will "rally to support us" into achieving our goals "without us really having to do anything."

At this point we haven't really done a whole lot to start working toward the goal. We've set a specific goal and allowed our minds to take note. It's kick-started the manifestation process. But then how do you proceed?

Follow Up with Action

The first step to take after beginning to think about your goal is to write it down. You can take a regular piece of paper, a sticky note, or a beautiful piece of stationery. Amber prefers something gorgeous for her and her clients. That way, you'll want to have it front and center all year. After all, it's more appealing to look at something beautiful, right?

Two important questions to keep in mind are:

1. *What is my goal for the year?*
2. *What am I working toward?*

Having a clear vision in mind will always help create a more straightforward path toward achieving your goals.

A goal is a "dream within a deadline," according to Amber. Once you've decided on the actual goal you're working toward, it's important to think about the specific times by when you want to meet your goal. "When do I intend to complete this goal?" is a question that should always be on the forefront of your goal setting.

Without a deadline, it can be tough to ensure that you follow up with your process and continue on the right path for reaching your goal.

The third step is deciding what and how much effort you intend to put forward. What will you give to attain this goal? This will kick off the universal law of reciprocity. This identifies what you are going to give in order to receive.

Finally, the last component of the goal setting process is to ask yourself what metric is associated with your goal. It's essentially figuring out how you will know when you've met your goal. One of Amber's best reminders is that we don't want to keep "going and going and going." You want to have something that is very clear so you'll know without a doubt that your goal can now be put to rest. You did it! Or if you did not quite get to where you wanted, you'll be able to figure out the next steps.

Align Your Goals with Your Life Values

The closer your goals align with your beliefs, your values, and your life, the better chance you have to achieve them. When Amber sits down to plan out her goals, she always makes sure that they are in line with where she is currently and where she wants to be a few months down the road.

Don't worry about keeping them neat and tidy! On Amber's goal cards you'll find her goals written out on the left side and on the right, a couple of things she keeps on her mind throughout the goal setting process. She says instead of just thinking of your goals "in a vacuum," think in terms of "where do I want my life to be?" instead.

Reflecting is also a huge part of setting goals for your life. Ask yourself a lot of questions. Amber suggests a few in particular:

- *How did the last year go?*
- *What do I want to change?*
- *Where did I feel really loved?*
- *Who do I need to bring more of into my life?*

Any sort of reflective question is going to ultimately benefit your goal setting experience—and outcome! And if you own a journal, use it. Reflecting in the form of journaling is a proven way to boost your thought process and organize your internal thoughts. It's one thing that Amber is glad she was forced to participate in while working toward her MBA. Even though you won't be graded on yours, it's still a great tool to use when planning what you want to achieve.

However, perhaps the most important question to ask yourself, Amber explains, is: Who do I want to be?

If you're setting goals that are too high or unrealistic, chances are you're going to feel "out of whack" with your core values that you reflected upon earlier.

For example, if you set a revenue goal of $5 million, you'll end up feeling frazzled and overworked, and not basking in the feelings of ease that you want to associate with your goals. So, really think through who it is you want to be when working toward them, not just how much money you want to be making.

Set Specific Times to Check In

For Amber, it's the ocean breeze in her Maryland hometown that reminds her that it's time to refresh her goals. There's something about the relaxing summer months that make you want to sit back, unwind, and make sure the goals you set are still on the right track. It's the ideal time to reflect, review, and revise the goals you previously wrote down.

As for the time she actually sets the goals, it's "100% in December." It's the end of the year and the perfect time to check in on everything that you want to improve upon for the coming year—a fresh start, if you will.

Amber emphasizes that it's crucial to hold yourself accountable for "showing up" for your goals. Is it how you want to be showing up? Are you showing up enough? You're the only one who has the power to consciously (and subconsciously, as we discussed before) make sure your goal process is operating smoothly. And if not, take the time to redirect.

The 90-Day Planning Model

Let's face it: Goals can be challenging. But that shouldn't be something you let hold you back. Instead, figure out a plan to help you achieve them in an organized and scheduled manner.

Amber swears by her 90-day planning model. It's something that she says she needs absolutely in place in order to reach her set goals. It's important, though, to remember that things can change. You can't plan every single detail because you never know what could be happening by next year (or even next week, in some cases)!

Planning three months is a lot more realistic than trying to plan for an entire year. "Things will happen with the kids; things will change in the market. Thing will change for my clients so I'll need to deliver or do something different and pivot," stresses Amber. Don't be weary of change. Embrace it.

Plan in the 90-day cycle and work with it. It helps considerably when you're having second thoughts or feeling pressured from the goals you set. It can feel a bit uncomfortable at first, but you can't let that stop you. Always come back to "Why did I set this goal?" This ties into the reflections you did before making these goals and helps to remember your vision behind them.

We all have those little voices that nag at us in the back of our minds. However, it's important to keep them right there: in the back of your mind. It's normal to experience doubts and second thoughts. They only emphasize how important it is to have your plan in place.

Here are some example of the questions of doubt you might encounter:

- *Is this the right time?*
- *Am I showing up to the game too late?*
- *Who wants to hear from me on this topic?*
- *Will I really make a difference?*

The answers are simple: Yes, you're doing the right thing. People do want to hear from you. And it's never too late to show up to the game. When you have a plan, it's easier to go back to it and put those second thoughts to rest.

When those questions come up, Amber heads straight back to the 90-day plan. Remember: You've got goals, you've got values, and with the plan you're ready to work toward achieving them every day.

Go Easy on Yourself

It's not always going to be smooth sailing. Just like we talked about not planning specific details a year in advance, sometimes the day-to-day hustle can shift and throw your plan off course. This is something that Amber has had to deal with in her own goals and at times with clients, too.

Before you kick, scream, stomp your feet, and cry—a reaction Amber says was close to her own in the beginning—think about the final goal. At the end of it all, does it really matter if one day gets thrown off schedule? No. What matters is that you're aligned with your values and you're showing up for what's most important in your life.

You'd give this sort of leniency to a client or friend. So why not give yourself the same benefit of the doubt? It's easy to say, "Of course you didn't get that done, and that's okay" to a fellow professional, but we need to learn to say that to ourselves. If you'd give your friend a break, give the same to yourself.

In the last few years, Amber has learned to leave harsh self-criticism behind, and it's been a total game-changer. It's brought a lot more joy and ease to her life—and doesn't that make the whole goal setting scenario that much easier to tackle?

Giving Yourself Time

The goal setting process works so well that as long as the thoughts are there in your mind, you'll naturally start taking baby steps toward them. Even if it doesn't work out exactly according to plan, there's always time to ensure it does. One quote that Amber keeps in mind, however, is "Planning is everything, but plans are useless." She says it's all part of going through the process. You've set the intentions, they're clear, and now you need to decide your priorities.

Remember to create space for the things that matter. Amber is a believer that at the end of the day, things are ultimately going to work out the way they're supposed to. Gift yourself that space.

Something Amber recalls being all too familiar with is frantically trying to cram every task for the week into the weekend. But if you just write everything down, there's no reason why you can't get everything done quickly and easily come Monday morning. "The week is just fine," explains Amber.

Allotting yourself enough time—or the right amount of time—is another necessary piece of the goal setting equation. If you set five days to complete something that you could realistically finish in two, chances are you're going to take the whole five.

Amber recommends writing a list of tasks and set a specific time to get each of the tasks done. You'll be surprised at how productive you can actually be. Monday mornings are a popular time for Amber to work her productivity magic, but, of course, it's going to be slightly different for everyone.

Getting Down to the Goals

Ultimately, your goal cards are going to be what you look at all year. Keep them visible and keep them accessible to return to whenever you need a refresher. Having the plan at your fingertips comes in really handy when you can easily reach for it and review or remind yourself of why you started—and always keeping the end goal in mind. One of Amber's must-haves within reach is her financial target, to help stay on track with revenue goals.

A fun fact that she likes to come back to is that businesses with clear revenue plans "gross 60% faster than those who don't." And when it comes down to the money, honey, that means a lot. (That statistic is from the State of the Business Owner study in 2014.)

Before locking in your plan, make sure your numbers are in place. The revenue tool is a total must-have for all business owners who want to see their businesses thrive.

Improving Your Planning

Even if you suck at planning, you can't give up. There is hope! You can always improve and you can always get better. Year after year you'll improve your process and refine the way you tackle planning. This comes back to the reflection stage of goal setting. Reflect on the ways that your planning didn't go the way it was intended to last year, and figure out the tweaks you need to make it better this year.

According to Amber, there are "a variety of ways to plan," so if one doesn't work out, give another one a try.

Be open to trying new ways of planning and new things. It's difficult to improve yourself if you're constantly stuck in the same rut. A good way to think about this is "What's the easiest thing I can do to get this done?" This is one question that comes in handy for Amber when she's sorting through a more complex plan.

"Why do I have to know the whole thing that I'm going to do?" questions Amber. "I'm going to pick the first step—the easiest step that I can do."

Start with what feels the most "doable" to you and move from there.

Listen to Your Body

Finally, if your body isn't functioning right, how are you supposed to stay focused? You can't. Amber maintains that getting enough sleep is actually a very necessary part of the whole plan—especially when your goal includes other people.

Amber recalls a time where she needed to work on recording a few episodes for her podcast, The Modern CEO, but also really needed a nap (she chose to take a nap!). You need to set time for yourself to recover and be able to produce your best work. Listen to what your body needs. Sometimes you might need a quick siesta; sometimes maybe it's a massage. Whatever it is, check in with yourself and do what you need to do in order to operate at your highest.

lifestyle profile

My lifestyle right now is very much my kids. I was on a photo shoot recently and the photographer asked if I had something to hold. Usually I bring stuff to the photo shoot; we have props. And this time, we forgot all of that. So of course, in that moment, Harper (my two-year-old) needed something and I knelt down to her and she was like "Yes, Mom, I am your props" and she gave me a high five! She did everything that she needed to be to reflect my lifestyle.

There's really a lot that wraps around that. We go on adventures together. I love spending time at the beach, too. And there's this illusion of entrepreneurs working on the beach, but I want that to be my life.

Visualizing Your Ideal Life

What would really fill my heart? What would make me happy every day? Many people talk about and do an "ideal life" exercise. It's really simple: just envisioning what your ideal life looks like. From the minute you wake up, what are you doing? What do you see? What do you feel? To whom are you talking?

Any Indulgences?

I love green juice. Yesterday I spent $30 on juice, and I drank it all, and spent another $25 this morning. That gives me a little anxiety. I've got to rework my budget. When I'm making them at home it's not as much of an indulgence because it's more affordable and reasonable.

Another indulgence that I'm just coming into now, and this happens to be a little bit probably from being in California, is really taking better care of my skin. People make fun, like "Oh those Californians, they're really obsessed with their bodies." Yeah, but it's a better lifestyle; it's just a better way of being. I definitely stepped into a better place of self-care, but it does feel a little bit like an indulgence right now. There's a facial place that happens to be two blocks from me, so I'm going to go get a facial next week because Matt deserves to spoil me.

Reading Recommendation

My go-to recommendation that I regularly go back to is *Business Brilliant*. What the book talks about is the difference between self-made millionaires and billionaires, and how they think and how they show up. Lewis Schiff, the author of that book, who's now become a friend, did so much research. It's based on data. It's not just comparing and anecdotal, but it is hardcore research. The first chapter blew my mind and lifted my beliefs on "Do what you love and the money will follow." He's got a twist on that in there on the first chapter.

bio

Amber McCue, business operations expert, studied organization development in Johns Hopkins' MBA program, and founder of NiceOps, a modern business management and operations consultancy based out of Annapolis, Maryland.

McCue is the creator of several noteworthy programs and courses for busy and first-time business owners, including her signature How to Clone Yourself (which accomplishes exactly what it sounds like, sans sheep); the long-term, hands-on program Freshly Implemented, in which she acts as an outsourced COO for struggling small business owners; and her latest and greatest development, CEO School, a brand new way for smart business owners to stop letting their business run the show, and start running the show for themselves instead.

I plan because

it's how I hope to make an impact on the world and a legacy for my family.

– REINA POMEROY

NAME: **Reina Pomeroy**

MBTI PROFILE: **ENTJ**

Reina believes that entrepreneurs are Skyscrapers or Builders. We embody our vision for our lives and our businesses, or we embody the steps to get to that vision. Think of it this way: Skyscrapers have a hard time seeing the steps needed to get to the sky, while builders have a hard time seeing the sky—the place they will (or should aim to) be 10 years from now.

Reina's in the builder category. She has a hard time wearing "10-year binoculars" and imagining how her life or business might look that far down the road, but she makes a point of planning and goal setting anyway. That's because she believes being intentional is the best way toward any sort of successful life. As a business therapist and coach helping right-brained and heart-centered creatives, Reina is big on covering all her bases in goal setting. It's why she calls herself a biz and life coach: because the two rely on the health of each other.

Reina says, **"I want to create a culture in our online industry where women feel empowered and nurtured, so that they can do the work that they're most passionate about, that fuels them and lights them up the most."**

That's what inspires her to set goals, and that's what inspired her to help other entrepreneurs find a goal setting system that fits their rhythm.

The Wheel of Life

First and foremost, Reina's goal setting process involves deciding which areas of her life are satisfied and which are most important for her to satisfy. With a sheet of paper and pen, she creates her Wheel of Life: one circle divided into eight different slices, including self-development, education, business, romance, and spirituality, among others. For each item on the list, Reina assigns a number of satisfaction, from most satisfied to least satisfied. Determining where you're lacking and where you're excelling, she says, will show you where your wheel is out of alignment and could need readjustment.

However, these wheels of life aren't always black and white. Take the romance slice, for instance: You could have no partner or dating life and be happy with that. "It's not the void of that person," Reina says. "It's about how satisfied you are with or without a romantic partner."

On the other hand, if you rank something like your health and wellness as important, yet you aren't satisfied with it and have not been giving it the time and energy it needs, your goals need to be readjusted to make room for health and wellness.

The Quarterly Plan

Reina uses the Fresh Start Workbook by Amber McCue and PowerSheets by Lara Casey and the Cultivate What Matters team to set her plans in place each quarter of the year. Fresh Start is home to Reina's revenue plans, while her PowerSheets include monthly check-ins and things she needs to be intentional about in and outside of her business—including time set aside for personal activities such as ice-skating.

Even her team is involved in PowerSheets, setting their intentions for the year and resetting each quarter alongside Reina. She has sent separate copies to her team members as soon as the PowerSheets are released in November, requests that they complete them on their own and implement their goals for Reina + Co. At that point, the whole team reflects, projects, and plans their course of action for the next quarter.

Without quarterly planning and goal setting, Reina says she wouldn't be able "to stop the spin." If she doesn't plan, she feels there's always something amiss—some part of her life or her business she isn't tending to. She likes to know what work she has to do on a Friday afternoon or if she gets that Friday afternoon off to play.

The Weekly Plan

For those who take a while to get into the right mindset for a certain set of tasks, whether that's writing copy or interacting with clients, Reina's **week-on/week-off method** may appeal. She follows an A/B schedule, meaning that she works on one area of her business for the first week, followed by a different one the second week.

In her "on" weeks (A week), Reina carries out client calls and team calls. These are the weeks in which she's totally active with her communities. The "off" weeks (B week) are generally dedicated to content creation, such as writing sales funnel copy and recording podcast episodes. This helps for batch blog post creation especially, as it allows you time to get into a groove and stay there while you finish post after post.

Reina has what she calls "open projects" for each of these weeks, and constantly checks in on how those projects are coming along. She considers on a weekly basis how those "open projects" might need realignment due to the changing and shifting nature of business and of life. To help with her check-ins, Reina schedules a recap call with a friend each Friday. She calls these CEO Fridays, because they're when she combs through all the work she's accomplished over the past week. It's one way to stay accountable and to be encouraged by someone besides yourself.

Also on CEO Fridays, Reina schedules a check-in with herself. She fills out a Typeform about how her week went—"kind of like a report card," she says—on which she writes the weekly tasks that overwhelmed her, the tasks that excited her, the people she loves supporting, and the people who support her. "It's just where you dump it all out," she says. It might seem like a small report at the time, but by the end of the year, Reina has accumulated a folder of reports in her Gmail account that she can open and reflect upon in detail.

"It's a really powerful tool to be able to look back on the things that I was really struggling with." Equipped with her weekly CEO reports, Reina is able to compare her finances with her entrepreneurial highs and lows.

After each weekly report is done, she clears the slate completely. She cleans her desk. She comes back to her desk Monday ready to tackle a brand new week.

Saving Instagram for Later

When it comes to actually making her plans and setting her goals, like a lot of us, Reina needs quiet time—and sufficient brain-dumping materials.

"I need white space in my calendar," Reina says. "I need no due dates. I need no external expectations." Last but not least, she says, "I need my son out of the house."

Once she gets down to the goal setting process, it's all 8.5 x 11 sheets of plain paper, colorful markers, and doodling. There's no room for Reina to be Instagram-style pretty in this process. She lets all her thoughts flow, organizes them, and then sets her goals. If necessary, she says, presentation can be done later.

On hand are, of course, Fresh Start, her personal PowerSheets, and her team PowerSheets. She uses a whiteboard to track ideas and a 12-month calendar from Paper

Source, which can be used to jot down dates throughout her thought process.

Reina typically comes up with 12 goals for the year. Often, it'll be three per quarter because of this, but sometimes, she'll leave a few "blanks" in the year so that she has room to include fun, impromptu projects. These she calls the "fun extras," whether they're a result of collaboration or simply a "stroke of genius that pops up."

"I allow that to happen because I trust my intuition," Reina says. She wants parts of her year to happen organically, so she gives new opportunities the space and time to enter her life. She cautions that it's important to leave out the goals that aren't so important in your year and to say no to those opportunities that don't fit with your schedule or your vision.

To keep current on her goes, Reina uses the inkWELL Press Weekly Kickstart, a patterned paper tool with a blank spot on each day of the week, where she sets the top five tasks for her week. On the side, there's also room for her well-appreciated brain-dumping.

While it may seem like she uses a lot of tools, Reina says it's important not to be overwhelmed by the amount available—and by feeling like you have to use up every little bit of a tool. "I haven't filled in every page [of Fresh Start], and I'm okay with that."

When it comes to using tools for your own goal setting, Reina says, "Find the things that work for you."

Asking the Hard Questions:
Why Didn't I Reach My Goal?

Don't waste time dragging your feet after missing a goal, Reina warns. Give yourself a period to make a decision, and then drop that goal or nail it.

To do this, it's best to start with a basic assessment. Ask yourself a couple of key questions:

1. *Is it my fault I missed the goal? Did I slack on it?*
2. *How can I correct it or decide to let it go?*

Reina herself has been guilty of dragging her feet before. She put off and put off writing a book, continuously telling herself *I'll be done by the end of December. I'll be done by the end of January.* Finally, she was forced to realize what was stopping her: "It was me needing to decide that I was going to put that project on hold."

Sometimes, that happens. Often, the case is either a) you're not as excited about a project as you were before, or b) you're like Reina and have too many important projects on your plate to work on another. Concretely deciding to put a project on the back burner, as Reina did with her book, can be a tough thing to do as an entrepreneur. People have a tendency to take up any new and exciting opportunity, without realizing how that might affect their other projects.

Instead, you need to learn to say, "I don't have room for that right now. I'm going to do that in quarter four."

The Foolproof Plan

Regardless of your goal setting or planning tools, every entrepreneur needs to set themselves up for a foolproof plan to success. Channeling her inner Builder, Reina says it's crucial to break your plans down into steps—and then break those steps down into even smaller steps.

"I think typically when we're starting a project, there's so many cool ideas. We just need to dump it all out. Put it on a piece of paper," Reina says. "Let it be done."

After that, it's all about organization. Reina designs a mind map for this part, categorizing projects into the creation aspects, launch aspects, and so on. After the mind map is complete, it can be put into a time line format. Setting dates for certain aspects of a project can be an effective way to keep on track. If writing a book, for example, you might set a date to have each chapter's first draft complete.

"Having milestones along a big project is really helpful," Reina says.

From there on out, relentless follow-through is necessary. You have to work your tasks into subtasks so small you can complete them in 30 to 60 minutes, advises Reina. If you can't complete them in that neighborhood, chances are they're too big and don't belong on a to-do list.

"If it sounds something like 'Write a book,' that's not going to be the most helpful thing on your to-do list., right?" Reina says. Completing one draft of a chapter at a time, on the other hand, can be effectively completed. This allows you to get into the nitty gritty of a project and make tangible, constantly measurable progress.

Your Life Still Exists

The first time Reina completed her PowerSheets, in 2014, she didn't include her life outside her business. All of her sheets were business-related, because she effectively forgot she had a personal life that needed as much commitment as her company.

"I call myself the life and business success coach because I feel like business and life can never be truly separated," she says. Business cannot be discussed without life, as life always affects business. Sickness in your family, or financial issues at home or within your marriage impact the way you show up in your business. Reina learned the hard way that business and life are one in the same and that she needed to bring them together intentionally to satisfy her Wheel of Life.

"I make a purposeful effort to have both personal 'me' goals as well as home goals." She differentiates between personal and home goals because in her home, she fills the role of homemaker, wife, mom, and dog walker, among other hats she wears. If she doesn't piece those out, she becomes what she calls "a second-class" in her own mind. When she divides the personal from the home, she's able to feel no guilt for fulfilling personal activities like reading, and she's able to enhance the joy of her family when she sets aside home goals.

lifestyle profile

I'm a mom and a wife. Like a lot of moms/wives, I feel like I am responsible for keeping our family and home running. There are responsibilities that I don't know where I store them in my head, but I somehow manage! I work full-time in my business and feel lucky that I get to do what I love every day. I'm interested in making sure that the work that I love is something that will continue to give back and make an impact if I am to put my son in daycare out of the home every day.

I also have taken up a few hobbies that I have personal goals around! I set a goal in 2017 to learn how to ice skate, learn hand lettering, and take up photography and become proficient at using a camera.

Most Repeated Intention

My most repeated intentions are "do what you can with what you have" and "be present where you are present."

Superpower

I think my superpower is being Social Glue and also being a Human Highlighter. What I mean by that is as people are talking to me I highlight things in my head, like "This is what you're trying to say." My secret talent, that people might not know, is that I was in choir for many, many years and I also played the violin for about 12 years.

Most Admired Character Trait

My most admired character trait that I don't necessarily embody is patience. It's a virtue that I think is something that I'm constantly working on—but I don't necessarily have all of. I think that as a parent, it gets tested quite a bit. I see people who have it in spades and I don't necessarily—yet.

bio

Reina Pomeroy is a business coach, educator, and podcaster for the creative entrepreneur community. She is the founder and owner of Reina + Co, the Life + Biz Success Coaching® practice. As a former licensed social worker and event lanner, she brings a unique perspective to the industry. The Creative Empire Podcast has been featured prominently on iTunes and garnered the attention of *New York Times* bestselling guests.

Reina works with multi-passionate entrepreneurs to create sustainable and profitable businesses that support a heart-filled life. At the time of this printing, Reina lives in the Washington, DC, metro area with her husband and son (but they're always on the move).

I plan because

I want to be in charge of creating the world around me.

— TARA NEWMAN

NAME: **Tara Newman**

MBTI PROFILE: **INFJ**

No One Size Fits All

If anyone knows about setting goals, it's Tara Newman. After all, she has the academics to back it up. She has a degree in organizational psychology and has spent a lot of time working on motivation, goal setting, and strategy. Tara has dedicated her life toward this work in a corporate setting—developing organizations and high-performing teams and individuals.

"SMART goals are B.S. and it is not a one-size-fits-all solution," Tara explains.

There's no specific way to set goals. It is all going to depend on the individual person. For example, Tara is in favor of more traditional goal setting while she advocates for other people to try their hands at non-traditional styles.

"There's no right or wrong way in my books," she says.

One general thing you do need to have, however, is an idea or framework behind your goal. There are certain things that will help a goal come to fruition—and some that won't.

Attaching your goal to a dream or vision makes it a reality and not simply an aimless pursuit. For Tara, if your goals have energy behind them and are coming from a place of emotion and feeling, they're more likely to become a reality. They'll happen more quickly than if they're solely a goal for the sake of being a goal, and you won't struggle as much.

It Doesn't Matter What You Call It

Goals can have all kinds of different names. You can call them bucket lists, intentions, desires. At the end of the day, it doesn't really matter. Tara views the naming of goals as "irrelevant" and instead thinks your energy should be focused on actually achieving your goals.

However, she finds that a lot of clients have a hard time with this. They struggle with fitting goals into a certain time frame. It can feel too constricting—and then there's the fact of actually succeeding at the goals you set. "A lot of people that I work with have a greater fear of success than they do of failure," Tara states. "That really impacts your goals."

Setting a Vision

Tara believes that once you have a vision, you're good to go. At least, to begin with. She says that for her, setting a goal is like adding "the accelerant on the fire" to really get it going. It provides more structure and allows you to inform your decisions differently.

Goals help you get to that vision quicker. Tara says that all of her goals are "anchored to a vision" of how she wants to feel and what the success of that goal looks like to her.

"I'll sit there and, you know, experience achieving it, how I celebrate it, how I feel once I've achieved it, and that's really what I anchor into for success," she explains.

Goal Setting Mode

"I'm always in some form of goal setting mode," says Tara. When she sets a goal for the year—for example, a revenue goal—she will work on reverse-engineering it back to the first quarter. Once she has the preliminary steps set, she plans the first 90 days. Tara only plans 90 days at a time—sometimes even less than that.

"Sometimes I don't even make it into the first week before I ditch the plan and I'm resetting it," she admits.

Flexibility and adaptability are absolutely key when it comes to goal setting. Often, especially for creatives, having too much structure can be suffocating to the goal setting process. For this reason Tara creates a plan that can easily be revised, thrown out, and restarted.

Think of it like this: You set your goals in a 90-day container. Then you break that down into a monthly container. From there, you can focus on what you need to accomplish weekly and what you're working on daily.

Ask yourself: "What are my three goals for the day?" Roll out into the week, then into the month, and so on.

"80% of Goal Setting Is Reflection"

After you come to the end of a goal setting cycle, it's good to hit pause and reflect on the process. Relentless self-reflection is a massive part of goal setting, according to Tara.

Some things to reflect on include:

- *What's working?*
- *What's not?*
- *How can you improve moving forward?*

In this reflection stage, we need to take responsibility for our achievements and celebrate those successes. It's easy to push those accomplishments aside and keep moving forward, but without acknowledging that we've achieved part of what we want to, it can be easy to become dissatisfied.

However, it's equally as important to take into consideration what isn't working. What are the things that you need to take "radical responsibility" for? What didn't go the way you thought it would? What changes do you need to make? We need to understand these mishaps so we can leave them behind and move forward with our goal setting with a clean slate.

At the end of a 90-day planning cycle, Tara sits down and looks and what happened in those months. She asks herself questions like:

- *What were the areas of significance?*
- *What were the areas of change?*
- *What happened overall?*

- *What do I need to call myself out on?*
- *Did I get distracted too easily?*
- *Did I know a goal didn't feel right and yet continue to chase it? Why?*

Letting Things Go

It's part of Tara's practice every week to let something go. People tend to ask themselves, "Who do I need to become to achieve these goals?" However, it's not usually that you need to become more of something but less of something else. From there, you start small. Ask:

- *What am I going to give up?*
- *What's the one pervasive story that keeps on coming up?*
- *What do I need to change?*

Tara has given up the need to have all information, to always be right, and to prove herself to people. At the end of the day, it's made goal setting that much easier.

If something isn't working in terms of your goals, don't give up. Instead, try to find something that does. Tara gets her clients to make a list of everything they want to achieve in the next 90 days. Then, she gets them to use that list as a source of focus every day.

Not Making Your Goals

In Tara's mind, it's never a failure when you don't meet your goals. For her, it's all about the feeling you get when you set (or release) the goal. You didn't feel good about the goal? Okay, release it. Let it go and move on.

When you can let go of the attachment to a goal, that's the ultimate success. The whole point of goal setting for Tara is to feel good about your goals and their outcomes. A lot of the time it's not your goal setting in particular that feels bad for you, it's your approach and energy around the goal.

Tara says she works with a lot of ambitious and achievement-driven people who tend to "strangle-hold" their goals. "They grip so tight and they suffocate any kind of life that would come from this goal," she notes.

For example, say your goal is to fill a group program and you want to get 10 people. You spend all your time and energy hell-bent on getting these 10 people, and all you can think about is achieving that. You end up missing your entire journey. You miss the experience of having conversations with these people, inviting them into your program, hearing them, understanding them. You're losing out on getting joy from the goal process.

Intuition vs. Logic

Part of Tara's movement is asking people to step up, take on bold leadership, and understand that it's not a logical experience. "The most successful leaders have led their businesses to epic revenue, impact, and goals by embracing intuition, by making gut decisions," Tara says.

Acknowledging that your business is a projection of your experiences is an important step in your goal setting process. We also need to remember to trust our initial feelings and go with our intuition.

"Whether you're a creative or a straight-up human, intuition is not something that's fostered in us," she explains.

In today's society, we're made to believe that the more things you accomplish, the better. But just because you cross 20 things off your list, it doesn't mean they're the right things. "Just because you're achievement-oriented, or you're a high achiever, it doesn't mean you're successful," Tara says.

We need to start looking at our lives in terms of performance instead of achievement in order to achieve what we really want and need to.

Setting the Right Goals

The practical side of this is that we need to have clarity about where we're going and what we want to work toward. We need to be able to create something that we can bring to life.

A great exercise for creatives, Tara says, is to look ahead at the next three years. You need to think big and create your vision. This isn't the time to hold back.

Think about:

- *Is this goal big enough?*
- *How much can I really achieve in the next three years?*
- *What am I willing to receive in the next three years?*

It can be scary to think about far into the future, but getting over that fear will ultimately help you set the right goals. If you're feeling extra ambitious, try to think about 10 years. Who do you want to be in 10 years? Where will you be? What are you going to achieve?

From there, you can lean into your vision. "It could be your reason why, it could be your story, or it could be your mission. But have something that you anchor into," says Tara.

lifestyle profile

I'm a forever coach, even at home. I don't necessarily see my role as the mother; I'm the mother coach. I feel like I'm always in role in some way or another coaching my family, really listening to what they have to say, really asking my children the deep questions, never trying to talk *at* anybody. It really has impacted my parenting in a large way, and that's really what I'm doing at home.

I'm a mom to two kids. I have an 11-year-old, and I have an eight-year-old. I am in the throws of tween-hood, which is really challenging my coaching skills. I'm also super-vulnerable with my kids and my husband. I really believe that that's the way we ought to live. It's a lifestyle. I need to practice this stuff all the time, so always really having very vulnerable and real moments with those who are in my home or around me, my friends. That's the INFJ in me, and I really identify with being an INFJ in all aspects of my life. I'm an introvert. I am a homebody. I like the cozy things. I like a hot cup of tea and I like my space.

Source of Inspiration

My source of inspiration is the vision that ambitious people don't have to kill themselves for success.

An Indulgence?

An extra cup of coffee.

What's Your Secret Talent?

I'm a really good skier.

Tara's Food Philosophy

Eat real food.

bio

Tara Newman is a high-performance business coach, productivity guru, crossfit and coffee fanatic, and expert in organizational psychology who's been helping leaders reach their highest potential for two decades. Tara believes that grinding, lack of focus, and feelings of frenzy are an outdated way of working and that building sustainable, world-class businesses requires more flow than hustle. She's the founder of The Bold Leadership Revolution, where she trains the world's leaders to have the endurance to make an impact.

Tara has been featured on almost a dozen podcasts as well as *The Huffington Post*, *YFS Magazine*, *The Daily Burn*, and *The Perpetual You*.

I plan because if I don't do it, someone else will do it for me.

— COURTNEY JOHNSTON

NAME: *Courtney Johnston*

MBTI PROFILE: **ENFJ**

You don't have to be a natural goal-setter to become a successful one. Courtney Johnston, chief rebel and copywriter at The Rule Breaker's Club, is living proof of that. She's a life and business advisor and a copy whiz, obsessed with goal setting not because she loves it, but because she "sucks at it."

That philosophy might sound foreign to those of us who are prone to avoiding the things we're not good at (or don't harbor at least some affection for), but it's one Courtney prescribes to daily. She has a knack for pursuing the stuff she, well, *doesn't* have a knack for.

"I'm always obsessed with the things I'm not good at, but that I can tell are important," Courtney says. Case in point, she's super focused on systems—which, she says, leads people to think she's really good at systems. The truth?

She's more focused on *getting* good at systems. Fascination with the daunting is a key player in Courtney's success.

Unrealistic goal setting has followed Courtney throughout her business life, so these days she focuses on creating reachable, satisfying, and exciting goals. Repeatedly disappointed by incomplete goals in the past, she confronts herself and asks some crucial questions before setting new goals. She considers whether or not she'll reach her goals based on her own negative or positive experiences, as well as how those bigger goals might look broken down into smaller steps.

Courtney believes too many entrepreneurs—herself included—have dream-big mentalities. This is a good thing, but only if those big dreams can be made into small, achievable steps. It's important to consider how you might feel when you don't reach a huge goal, and how much better you might feel when you reach a realistic one. To her big dreams, Courtney asks, "What can I actually achieve in a shorter amount of time?"

Is it Realistic or a Stretch?

Like the saying by philosopher George Santayana goes, "Those who do not study history are doomed to repeat it." This, too, is the case in setting goals. Courtney has been in business for four years and says her unrealistic goal setting tendencies became apparent when she aimed to double her business revenue each year. **Each year, however, she found the goal too huge and experienced déjà vu disappointment come wind-up season.**

"I've never doubled my business," Courtney says. "Never."

While considering how she could make a more realistic revenue goal, Courtney discovered that she had increased her revenue by 1.5 times every single year, "almost to the cent." She thought, why double when she was already becoming significantly more successful each year? One and a half times seemed a reasonable and achievable goal, so she ran with it.

"That's realistic," she says, "and even if I go past it, that's really exciting." There's nothing wrong with leaving a little wiggle room at the finish line. In fact, it can provide greater peace of mind and an even bigger cause for celebration if your success surpasses your expectations.

Of course, going by the data means those who are brand new to the world of business or to even one area of business might feel like they have no place to start. A realistic goal needs a relative-to, so Courtney insists that it's OK to make a few mistakes, underestimate, or overestimate. Setting goals in any given area requires at least a little experience in it. She says, "You have to start where you're at and what you think you can really do, then be conscious that it's your first time goal setting in this domain."

Courtney suggests setting a goal for a short amount of time and seeing how it goes. "You might think, 'Okay, that was a lot harder than I thought,'" she says. She compares it to trying out a new workout routine: It can feel exciting and empowering for the first three days, but by the fourth day, it might be totally exhausting. That's when the intentions behind the goal need to be reconsidered, or the goal itself broken down into manageable steps.

Breaking it Down in Real Time

Courtney uses Natalie MacNeil's *Conquer Your Year* planner to break down her goals. A good planner like *Conquer Your Year* makes bigger ideas into tangible milestones before dividing them into small, specific actions for each month, week, and day of the year. Courtney compares the macro-to-micro method to going on a road trip: The total distance can look laboriously long on a map, but when it's split between restroom breaks and ice cream stops, it looks a lot easier.

"It gives me milestones and things I can do right now, versus feeling like the goal is really far away," Courtney says.

Courtney derived plenty of her break-down inspiration from the book *The 12-Week Year*. She plans her year in quarters as a reliable method to keep progress within sight. *The 12-Week Year* was written largely as a subversion to the typical business practice of gaining 11th-hour profit and momentum in the month of December. Authors Brian P. Moran and Michael Lennington presented the idea of making quarterly goals rather than yearly ones; quarterly goals allow businesses to maintain momentum throughout the year and avoid traditional last-minute scramble.

Courtney divides her quarterly planning into groups of 13. She says, "If you think about a 52-card deck, there's four suits of 13 cards each. The same thing with the year. There's 52 weeks divided into 13, that's four groups. I do 12 weeks sprints, and then…I just make sure that in [week 13], I have the plan for the next quarter."

Headspace Is Key to Quarterly Planning

A day off can make all the difference for mapping out a quarter. Courtney says her week 13 always involves at least one day off; otherwise, she's too caught up in the small stuff to tap into the big.

Imagine eagle-eye view versus ground view, or as Gary Vaynerchuck puts it, "the cloud and the dirt." Courtney says it's difficult to come from the mindset of "the dirt" (those small, necessary, day-to-day tasks) to "the clouds" (the big 12-week plans).

She says her cure for reaching the clouds is a day off. The space allows her to soar to eagle-eye view and get a clearer idea of what's right for her business before she sets her upcoming goals. She's fond of quiet spaces for this kind of goal setting, and in her ideal world, she says she would work in a room full of whiteboards, Post-it notes, and paint—and when she needed any tool for mapping out her goals, said tool would appear.

Of course, reality finds her often on an airplane with a Dollar Store notebook and a pen when quarterly planning takes place, so she brainstorms and free-writes on paper to allow her creativity to flow. She says she doesn't allow herself to get caught up in writer's block during that time. "Coal miners don't get coal mining block. They don't go into the coal mine and say, 'You know what, I'm just not feeling it today. I'm not inspired.'" The same goes for goal setting. "I have to get into a space where I'm letting go of where I am right now and thinking about where I want to be, and I find this to be true with my students as well," she says.

In Courtney's program, Yay for Clients, she encourages her students to look beyond the clients they have to clients they want to have—the people they want to serve the most. She says entrepreneurs have a habit of focusing on the client base they already satisfy and aiming all of their goals at those clients, rather than at the ones they truly desire.

"Don't make a business to suit these people. Make a business to get the people you want," she advises. She says this is the same with goals.

Before setting her goals, Courtney reflects on where she is in her business and tries to let that place go. She analyzes her emotions—the way she wants to see her business—while analyzing the facts and the numbers, before she works through a plan to bring those emotional wants to reality. "I negotiate between my desires and my business strategy brain," she says. That way, her goals remain realistic but heart-centered.

Measuring Goals Doesn't Always Mean Achieving Goals

Courtney's goals are already set in a measurable way. She says her main problem comes when she doesn't reach a goal and has to assess why. Sometimes, the goal is too ambitious (it covers too much with too little space) but other times, the goal simply isn't the right goal. She says this is the difficult part: figuring out why it wasn't the best course of action, and what the better one could be. A good comparison can be made to marathon running. Some people want to run marathons and will make it to the finish line. Others, like Courtney, won't make it to the finish line. And it's not because the goal is too ambitious; if it were, nobody would be able to finish. **Rather, it's because the desire to run is not present for some people.**

They have their own thing, and it just isn't marathon running.

Courtney says if you have to force yourself to like the goal because it's *your goal,* you need to realize it's the wrong one. Plenty of people base goals on what they see those around them doing. "It's a lot easier to pluck a goal from the Internet, like 'Everybody wants 1,000 Instagram followers. I'm going to do that, too.'" Courtney says this is the kind of wrong-intention goal setting to avoid. "Maybe you hate Instagram," she points out. In that case, you shouldn't do it.

For a long time, she says she was committed to the idea of breaking six figures. She kept falling short of the goal and feeling bad about herself, before she realized it was the goal's fault, not hers. Courtney asked, "Why am I setting this goal? Do I even need this goal?" and stepped away from the obsession with six figures. Six figures would come later, when she followed the right path and didn't strive for an unnecessary number.

Courtney says setting the wrong goals is almost always an unhealthy move. "I think a lot of us set the goal and the goal becomes our keeper. The goal is punishing us." It's important to remember that the goal doesn't own you—you own the goal.

Goal setting is more about discovering what you truly want and making a realistic plan to reach that vision than setting goals you believe you should be setting. However much of a messy, trial-and-error process pursuing the right goals can be, it's the best one.

Courtney says, "That's the only way to achieve a goal, I think."

Plan for Life to Get in the Way

"Life gets in the way. How would it not?" Too often, Courtney sees people who set goals without taking into account life's inevitable and unpredictable motions. "You will have crises, you will change your mind, someone will get sick. Every time you reach a new height things are going to happen."

Courtney plans with the knowledge in mind that unexpected things will interrupt. She says this is another way to keep goals realistic. "Every time I set a goal, I plan for a million things to try to stop it." Goals should not be set for a perfect life, or even a life moving at the pace it is right now. Goals should be set around possible financial crises, health crises, and mental breakdowns. Plan for all three, and your goals will be the most reachable.

"If you want to have an upper hand, plan for terrible things to happen and you will start to achieve your goals," Courtney says.

The Rebel at Heart: Keeping the Personal Flexible

In the first few years of business, most have to sacrifice a little or a lot of their personal lives to growth. Hustling is required to get clients and customers and build a solid brand, and Courtney is no stranger to entrepreneurial overwhelm.

"You have to be crazy," she says. Devoting plenty of time

and energy into your business becomes a habit after several years. Courtney recently took a trip to Algeria and says it was the first time in a long time she has had to slow down and disconnect from WiFi.

She tries not to follow a rigid, measurable goal setting plan in her personal life. She's more of a "did some exercise each day this week" kind of goal setter than a "how much body fat did I lose this week?" one, and she prefers to keep it that way. In her *Conquer Your Year* planner, she tries to include a fun element on her daily to-do list and meditate for five minutes each day. But in the end, Courtney is a rebel, a lover of the unorganized personal life, and aims for a future that will constantly inspire her and bring her closer to the outcomes she truly wants.

lifestyle profile

Favorite Hour of the Day

I like late mornings. I love 11:00 a.m. because it's coffee drinking and conversation time. That is my favorite thing—holding my mug and talking to people and waking up.

Biggest Indulgence

I don't believe in being guilty about pleasure. Indulgence and pleasure are everything to me. I would say things that come to mind are things like long showers, really, really good dark chocolate, really good aged cheeses, sleeping in, and buying plane tickets. Also, watching comedies on Netflix. That's what my boyfriend and I do now: We just watch comedies.

Food Philosophy

Pleasure! I feel like it's confusing to people because when I say pleasure, someone would be like "donuts." I eat a donut once a year and that's pleasure. But if I had a donut every day, it would not be enjoyable. It's about whole foods. I love whole foods. I can actually feel the energy of them. I would say colorful foods, too.

bio

Courtney Johnston is the founder and copywriter at The Rule Breaker's Club where she teaches women how to create and sell signature services that stand out from the crowd! She's pretty much the only person who can make writing sales pages fun (hint: It involves rainbows and pots of gold). Courtney has been featured on Inc.com, CreativeLive, and *The Huffington Post*. She's from Michigan, started her business in Paris, and currently lives in Vancouver. You can learn her 14-part sales page recipe for free at RuleBreakersClub.com.

I plan because

I want this business and my life to live longer than me

– JILLIAN SMITH

NAME: _**Jillian Smith**_

MBTI PROFILE: **ESFJ-A**

As an event planner, Jillian Smith knows what it means to be organized. That's why she follows the mantra "You don't have to get ready if you stay ready," so new leaps and bounds (and even setbacks) in business won't take her off-guard. Jillian's been a lifelong organizer and lover of events, and when she left her corporate job at 32 years old to pursue her real passion of event planning, she knew she had to make a plan for her *own* dreams.

Those dreams, Jillian discovered, aren't all to do with business. They involve reaching for success in every aspect of your life.

The Magic Number

Jillian's favorite number is eight—but that's not what prompted her to break down her life into eight goal setting categories. She knew she needed time in her year for those things that enriched her life, and so she wrote them into her yearly plan alongside her business goals. Here's how Jillian's yearly planning looks (in no particular order):

1. *Friends and family*
2. *Health and wellness*
3. *Business*
4. *Relaxation/vacation time*
5. *Spirituality*
6. *Self-development*
7. *Financial planning*
8. *Romance*

She touches on what she wants to see happen in each category during the year, then moves into quarterly planning to set tangible goals for those visions. A trip to San Francisco, for instance, is often enough to rejuvenate her for client work, meshing health, vacation time, and business together to make things happen in a positive way.

Jillian says goal setting is the only way to manifest your ideas. "It's easy to have a thousand different ideas," she says. Goal setting helps prioritize those ideas and work the important ones into reality. Setting a priority list is essential for Jillian and for her team at OneTouch Events. It prevents them from veering off course at any given time.

That kind of priority setting, Jillian adds, helps keep you on track when unpredictable things happen. She uses the weather as an analogy: Some years, you're wearing flip flops in January and Uggs in April. **Your prioritized goals should be set so that even when the weather catches you off guard, you know your course and you stick to it.**

"It also helps me to be the best leader I can be, because I do have a team and they look to me to provide them with guidance," Jillian says.

Post-Its and Whiteboards

A good old-fashioned calendar, notebook, pen, and oversized sticky notes keep Jillian on track for her year. All her big goals are designated for the giant sticky notes, which are stuck on the wall to serve as a constant reminder. When she's reached a milestone, she has the satisfaction of crossing it off and knowing she's one step closer to that sticky-note goal.

She makes good use of PowerSheets for the nitty-gritty details. PowerSheets include the day-to-day tasks that can be checked off on the way to a bigger goal. For that reason, Jillian says PowerSheets have been "the most rewarding product" she's invested in.

She adds that meeting with an accountability buddy (or buddies) can work as a motivator to accomplish monthly tasks. Jillian feels far more guilty when she has to announce to her group of girlfriends that she hasn't met her goals for the month, than she would simply saying it to herself. That sense of accountability fuels her to succeed.

Big on categories in every aspect of her business and

life, Jillian uses categorization to decide on priority goals. Once she has these visions all written down, she deciphers patterns and the things that need tending to in her life. By writing down her business priorities last year, for example, Jillian realized she did not have enough time to see her parents and that this goal would have to become a priority. To do this, she stuck to a smaller number of clients, thereby prioritizing her parents on her goals list.

She believes it's necessary to ask yourself: *What is most important to me, and what can be tangibly done within my time frame?*

Taking a Step Back: The Ideal Goal Setting Season

For Jillian and her team, business peaks from the spring until the fall. Close to the end of the year, they experience a quieter time and can come together as a team to think through their year and what they want to see for the next year. She says it often takes several months for the team to decide what worked and what didn't during the year, and how they will respond to that. **Jillian takes cues from her team, acknowledging what they desire to do so that they can be their best, most successful selves.**

To take this "step back" and plan for the next year, Jillian time-blocks, a method of productivity she describes as "key" for any task at hand. "You can work on 12 or 13 different things at the same time, but by multi-tasking, you're not putting that laser focus on anything," she says. Time-blocking is something she implements on a daily basis. It's a pin-sharp way to produce the best work, best prioritizing, and best planning.

This doesn't mean that Jillian doesn't have multiple projects on the go. She does; however, she blocks out time to intentionally work on each of them, and ensures that if more than two major initiatives try to make it into her life, they are moved into the next quarter.

Reigniting and Remixing Your Goals

Those who overachieve know what failure feels like: huge. Jillian used to beat herself up over missing goals, but has since learned to take a more reasonable and considerate approach. Failing without deeply considering the reason for that failure is *the best way to continue failing.* You have to take a step back and ask why something happened and how it might not happen again. **Was the goal obtainable? Why or why not?**

If the goal *was* attainable and you simply weren't physically, mentally or emotionally there to achieve it, then it's time to "reignite that goal in the same context," Jillian says. But if that goal wasn't obtainable outside out those reasons, it's time to "remix" it for the real world. "Maybe that goal was a little lofty. Let's bring it down a couple notches," she says.

Describing herself as oftentimes "bull-headed" and determined to reach goals that perhaps aren't immediately achievable, Jillian says her clients have helped her realize the value of flexibility in business. You need to be able to pivot at a moment's notice, for your own sense of accomplishment and for your realistic, professional success.

Accepting When Your Goals Are Reached, or Finished

Jillian's checklist decides when she's reached her goals or not. Having a strong project management background, she's familiar with the planning scheme of overall picture, critical path, and milestones in between. Her process includes a big business goal like *rebranding,* with check-offable steps like *selecting a logo and website designer* and *creating business cards.*

When she hits each of her milestones, she knows she is reaching her big goal.

However, sometimes the goal will begin to feel unimportant, Jillian warns. As hard as it can be, it's okay to drop a goal mid-year. "Just because I said it in January doesn't mean I have to continue with it," Jillian says. As life continues to happen and your business evolves in different, positive ways, some goals can become irrelevant. When this happens, it's good to be flexible and let that goal go. If you're determined to have disappointment in your life, you'll continue to beat yourself up over dropping goals. If you are instead determined to have little disappointment in your life, you allow yourself reprieve and a sense of fulfilment.

"Focus on retooling for what you have next."

Even if the goal isn't a bad one, Jillian adds, it's important to drop some if you have too many on-the-go. She compares her brain to a web browser with too many tabs open. "Give yourself permission to close those tabs."

When you don't close those tabs, your business projects

can keep you up at night and take a toll on your family, social, and personal lives. Everything has a downstream effect, and if you don't figure out how to turn off sometimes, Jillian says you will, quite simply, "go crazy."

There's No Wrong Way to Plan

Jillian confesses that she isn't a fan of Planning Pod, an online event-planning software. She used to feel crappy about that, because she listened to all the female entrepreneurs around her raving about how useful and great it was, but she never enjoyed nor benefitted from it.

"We can easily get caught up on what's hot, what's now, what's trending, what I'm supposed to be doing," Jillian says. But that's not the right way to plan. The right way to plan is the way that, plainly, *feels right*. The way that's absolutely for you.

"If writing out [your goals] on little bitty sticky notes and posting them on a wall works for you, that works. If you need to rent a conference space and have a whiteboard, that works. If you are an app person and you just want to type it out, that works," Jillian says. **There is no wrong way to plan. Get focused and make things happen in your own life.**

Plan for Her Peace of Mind

Life will throw all kinds of things in your way. It's inevitable, no matter who you are or what type of business or home life you lead. If you don't have a plan, you won't be able to respond to the weather and keep on track. This can lead to a quitter's mentality and, all too often, abandoned businesses. Jillian says having even just a skeleton of a plan is better than having nothing at all.

"I plan because I want to be a success and I plan because I want this business and my life to live longer than me," Jillian says. "This is generation planning, and not just for today."

lifestyle profile

My non-business lifestyle is pretty boring—I'm working on it. One of the things I struggle with is that my business became my life for a few years because I was doing this while I still worked full-time. Now I've gotten into a rhythm of what it takes to run the business. I'm incorporating working out and hanging out with friends more!

Food Philosophy

You should eat to live, not live to eat. However, you only have one life, so you need to eat what you want, and then just work your ass off in the gym! I love to eat really rich. I'll try something at least once. I never thought I would love escargot but I [tried it] when I was in France and we ate it every day after. It's all about being adventurous in life and knowing that you might have to add an extra day of working out—but just not over-indulging.

Most Admired Personality Trait

I don't like to brag a whole lot on myself, but I have been told that I'm very thoughtful. So, thoughtfulness, because that can transpire in both your personal and your professional life. I've been told that I have a knack for reading the energy of other people, too. Being able to read people's energy—and playing off of that energy—is really important because we're in a client-based business, so you kind of have to change your personality type to fit with who you're working with.

bio

Jillian's love of entertaining dates back to high school, when she planned holiday parties with her friends. As time went on and she honed her skills, she planned and hosted a wide range of events, from specialty theme parties to intimate group functions and beautiful weddings to professional corporate events. Knowing she'd found the secret sauce to planning successful events, Jillian decided to take the leap from her corporate job and began marketing her services outside her network of friends and relatives to launch OneTouch Events.

Her approach to event planning is simplicity. She takes cues from you to package the personality and feel of your event into something that is uniquely you. She's drawn to the streamlined, sleek approach to executing a grand affair, and infuses technology and planning tools into her events—for a simple and effective process. She pairs her right-brained organization with her creative left brain for the perfect event and biggest "wow" factor.

I plan because

I never want to grow stagnant.

– JENNA KUTCHER

NAME: *Jenna Kutcher*

MBTI PROFILE: *ESFP*

Jenna Kutcher is one of the most relatable people you'll ever meet. She works most days from her couch in her yoga pants with her two rescue pups in her lap. She's a wedding blogger, artist, podcaster, educator, and self-proclaimed mac-and-cheese connoisseur. In 2011, she left her corporate job to pursue her dreams — and she hasn't looked back since.

Consequently, she's had to become an excellent goal setter as well. Branching out and working on your own takes a lot of focus, determination, and goal setting abilities. Whether they're carefully thought out and set in stone, or more go-with-the-flow, goals are an important part of being an entrepreneur.

Jenna's approach to goal setting is to "set big picture goals and let the little stuff work itself out." In other words, she doesn't sweat the small stuff. She realizes that goals are constantly changing and evolving, and adjusts her goal planning accordingly.

"I like to do more quarterly goals vs. annual because half the stuff I'm doing right now I wouldn't have dreamed of [last year]," she says.

As your path twists and turns, all you can do is readjust your goals and help them fit in with your life as it's happening now.

The Desired Outcome

For Jenna, the whole purpose of setting goals is to make sure you're moving forward in your life. And how do you measure that success? "I am laser focused on metrics and numbers," she says. By keeping track of your "success data" you can ensure that you're moving forward and staying on the right path.

Set normal goals, achievable goals, and "big, scary goals," too. There's no such thing as dreaming *too* big. With the right determination, ambition, and goal setting tools, anything is possible.

The Goal Setting Time

Usually, when you're starting a new project you want to have some goals in place to make sure it's successful. We all have goals and dreams for every new project we're working on, which come with direction and being able to see the bigger picture of your business.

Every few months, Jenna is pushed to set goals. It

happens naturally then and she works with it. "I like it project-based because then it's not like you're sitting down trying to figure out what your entire year is going to look like, it's less overwhelming, and I'm more likely to set big, big goals," she explains.

Setting goals right off the bat when you start something new will set the guidelines, hopes, dreams, and everything in between to make your project a success!

Assessing Your Success

Looking at metrics give you a clear yes or no answer in terms of whether or not you hit your goals. If you're a numbers person, like Jenna, the numbers give you a solid answer on your outcome. Along with the numbers, take a look at your feelings. Are you still feeling passionate? Inspired? Focused? If not, it's time to tweak your goals to get your feelings back on track.

Setting little objectives throughout the course of a project is something Jenna finds useful. When you're working in advance, you have time to review your progress and check out the pieces of your goal puzzle. Are they all fitting together? Are they adding value to you moving forward?

Jenna sets three types of goals: good, better, and best.

"Good means you're satisfied with your outcome, better means you're super stoked and popping bubbly, and best means you'd run a naked lap around your house screaming because you just did the biggest thing ever!" she says.

Goal Setting Tools

Utilizing tools in your process further solidifies your dedication and commitment to your goals. Jenna has a "trusty little notebook" in which she writes her goals. Putting your goals down onto paper helps you to realize them as real, important projects. If they're just in your head it can be easy to forget about them or push them aside.

Jenna also keeps a detailed account of her goals in Google Drive docs so she can review each goal, every project, and every account for each success. When everything is organized and written out, it's much easier to track your progress and see where you are.

Another secret weapon Jenna uses is a "big, messy spreadsheet" of all the subconscious things she's been working on: "the one you wouldn't want anyone to find because you'd feel silly or trivial but it's really what you want," she says.

When Life Gets in the Way

When Jenna doesn't meet a goal, it's usually because she's moved on to a new project. However, there are times when she finds peace in "falling short" of her goals. (Seriously.) Sometimes your motives change or your direction takes on a whole new route.

When life gets in the way of your goals, try not to let it hinder your process. If you're working far in advance of your goals, you always have the option of getting back on track. Jenna tries to be at least two months ahead of schedule on all her big goals so that when life does hit the fan, she has dedicated recovery time.

Why Jenna Plans

The number-one reason why Jenna plans and sets goals is to never become stagnant in her life. "One of my biggest fears is going through life in autopilot," she explains. That's why she's always aiming to be inching forward through different channels, avenues, and plans.

She always strives to be reaching toward something, whether it's her set goals or a completely new plan. Jenna doesn't believe that we were made to just be content in this world. Her belief that there is more to life pushes her forward each and every day.

lifestyle profile

Jenna is married to her husband, Drew, and loves hanging out with their two pups, Chloe and Tucker. Most weeks, she co-works with friends in an office — well, when she's not traveling for work one week out of every month. Fitness is really important to Jenna, too; she works out at the Crossfit gym every morning. (Now that's what we call dedication at its finest!)

Most Repeated Intention

I am enough. I am enough. Seriously, that's it.

Source of Inspiration

What is currently interesting me. I think I like to watch a lot of things happening and something will spark my interest, but it takes me some time and processing to take action on a new idea. I like to really be thoughtful, make sure I'm super invested, and be ready to defend it (which means I actually care). I think I carefully consume content and then challenge myself to make it better or my own.

Secret Talent

I have the ability to fall asleep instantly on a plane, like before we even take off, and I can sleep the entire flight no matter if it's two hours or 10. It's amazing (also highly unproductive!).

Most Admired Character Trait

My ability to take action. When I want something I just do it. I've lost the filter to question myself or dwell. I just go for things and it's definitely my best trait because that is how I get so much done. No second-guessing; just do it.

bio

Jenna is small-town Wisconsin photographer, painter, and educator with big dreams. Obsessed with: mac and cheese, puppies, and yoga pants. Most days, you'll find her in yoga pants, working on the couch with a smile on her face and rescue pups in her lap — or making googly eyes at her hunky husband Drew from across the room. She's a wedding photographer, podcaster, a watercolor artist, and an educator — plus, she's always got her bags packed for her next wheels-up adventure.

I plan because

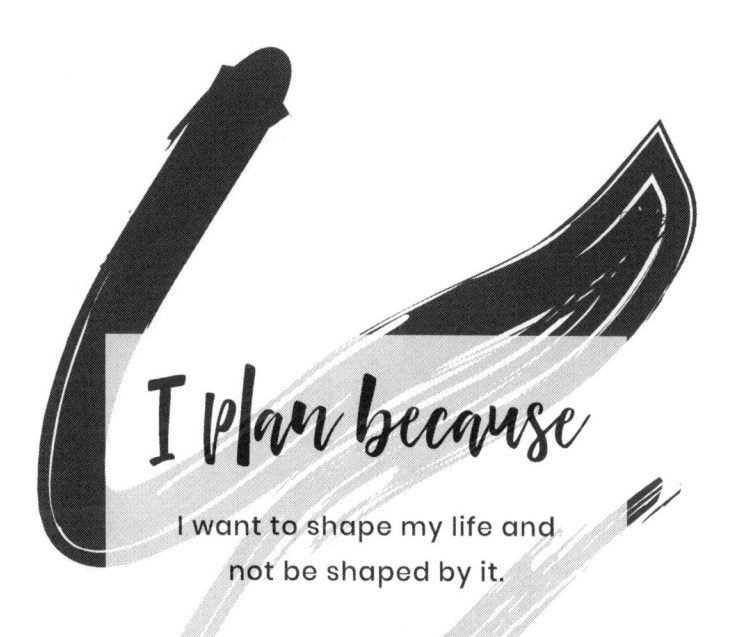

I want to shape my life and
not be shaped by it.

– LISA JACOBS

NAME: __Lisa Jacobs__

MBTI PROFILE: __INTJ__

The Five Pillars of Life

When it comes to setting goals, Lisa Jacobs is as thorough as it gets. Starting with one big picture, she breaks it down into categories: mental, spiritual, relational, financial, and physical. "I don't really separate business from personal life," she says. After all, she *is* the business.

Lisa is a busy mom of four, married for 20 years, and a female entrepreneur with her own marketing business. All things considered, it's truly important to set time aside for goal setting—especially when all areas of your life tie into similar goals.

So, the idea of the "five pillars of life" all comes down to being grounded in all these ways in order to meet business, personal, and financial goals.

The first thing Lisa likes to ask herself is: What do I want to change? Once you've decided your initial goal, some of the following questions could be:

- *How am I going to make that different?*
- *How am I going to be even more excited to wake up every day in the coming months and the coming year?*
- *What am I going to do differently?*

Then, you can start to turn those thoughts into quarterly, monthly, weekly, and daily goals and tasks. It's important to be thorough here since there are so many categories. Break down the big picture and funnel it into the tasks you're going to complete daily, monthly, and so on.

"Everything I do, especially for work, has a purpose," states Lisa.

The Desired Outcome

For Lisa, the desired outcome of setting goals is all about self-improvement. "I think self-improvement, self-enhancement, and excellence is just delicious," she says. "I'm in love with all those things." And what better motivation than that?

You always want to be moving forward. It can be hard to feel like yourself if you're not constantly moving forward and reaching towards your goals—especially if you're a motivated person. When it comes to goal setting, you should always be thinking about moving forward.

If there's something you don't like in your life, change it. If something is bothering you, eliminate it. Life is too short to live with things that don't make you happy! "What have I been struggling with for entirely too long?" is a question that Lisa often asks herself.

Set Goals Every Day

When asked about a specific time of year or day that Lisa sets goals, her response is simply "I goal set every day." She does, however, reserve the week between Christmas and New Year's to figure out the year's plan. According to Lisa, it's a "fabulous" week for goal setting because there's nothing she absolutely *must* do except reflect and set goals.

Use that time to really think about what you achieved during the year and what you could improve upon. Make it a goal to spend this whole week breaking down tasks, goals, dreams, and everything else you want to tackle. Lisa uses this week to do a seven-day segment on her blog, laying out what she's working on each day.

Breaking Down Your Goals

Breaking everything down, into the categories mentioned before, will help immensely with keeping yourself on track and organized in your goal setting. For example, one of Lisa's "spiritual" goals is to settle her mind from anxious thoughts and procrastination.

So, she came up with a few small tasks that can help her work toward this goal every day. They range from acupuncture, hot baths, gym time, or even something as simple as a meditation app that reminds her to calm her mind.

With each goal broken down quarterly with tasks to complete and cross off from the list along the way, it's easy for Lisa to stay on track and see exactly where her progress is. In order to achieve everything, you need to really create change. Everybody wants change, but only a small percentage of people genuinely see the changes they want to see. Lisa says she truly strives to be in that percentage, every day of her life—no matter what.

Goal setting Tools

Lisa warns against letting yourself slip away from your goals. She confesses, "When I walked away from it for a couple days, I found that within a few weeks I was back to my old habits: drinking wine, watching reality TV, and expanding my waistline versus working toward my fitness goals, which are totally different than that."

Consistency is key—and so is using tools to help you stay on track. Lisa uses her daily planner to keep detailed notes and checklists that she reviews every morning. The only digital tool she utilizes is Asana, which helps team members manage progress and projects.

Going back to paper, another weapon of organization Lisa favors is a bullet journal by Scribbles That Matter. And that's besides her collection of everyday planners! "If I see a day planner, I can't *not* buy it," she admits.

Being able to keep detailed notes, doodles, and checklists organized into a daily planner is an essential tool for staying on track with your goals. And an added bonus? Being able to show off some of your progress on Instagram.

Setting Goals in Front of an Audience

Back in 2013, Lisa started vlogging about her goal setting week in between Christmas and New Year's. The whole experience of publicly setting goals was a very personal one. She was able to connect on a deep level with her audience. However, she didn't feel like it always held her accountable. She didn't find herself always achieving her goals—but that's okay.

It's all about the personal review and reflection. It's okay not to achieve your goals by your specific dates. It just means that you need to take a step back and figure out why. Revise your plan and make the necessary changes to get to where you need to be.

Keep Moving Forward

When it comes to business, Lisa is all about making financial goals. She is constantly striving to do better, something that she came to learn from doing her income reports for her newly launched business. She figured out that she had made the same amount of income ("not a penny more, not a penny less") for four years in a row and decided that something had to change.

According to Lisa, she was stalled and stuck. "What kind of businessperson am I if I don't know how to grow this salary?" she remembers asking herself. "What kind of limitations do I have?"

Goals become even more important in your life when you reach one of these stagnant times. Growth is essential.

However, how can you be growing when you're not evolving your plan and moving forward?

Some questions to ask if you find yourself in a position like this could be:

- *How far am I from where I want to be?*
- *What tools or education do I need to breach that distance?*
- *What steps can I take to literally move myself forward?*

Once you've made a commitment to get ahead, it'll be easier to keep moving in the right direction. In Lisa's words: "If we're not moving, we're not making anything happen."

Your Best Year

Every year Lisa publishes a book called *Your Best Year* and every year it changes. It evolves—as will you, in time, as you set your goals and work toward achieving them every single day.

The idea behind *Your Best Year* is to set a main goal and figure out the profit strategy and the growth strategy. After all, every working hour you put into your business should be counting toward something. Whether it's income or growth, it doesn't matter. What matters is that you're focused and ready to take on the tasks at hand in order to expand your business and accomplish your goals.

If your plan is to grow your income, you need to set your dollar amount and figure out the steps to get there. For example, if you know that revenue comes from your emails, you need to set a goal of raising your email list. From there you can come up with the necessary steps to achieve that.

Some points to consider:

- *If emails equal revenue, you need fresh content.*
- *Every Thursday you could write a new blog post to send out in the emails.*
- *At 9 a.m. sharp on Friday mornings you can send out the email.*
- *Every day you can spend time engaging on social media to remain relevant and create movement with your customers.*

However, it's important to set out the exact steps you're going to take. This is something a lot of people miss out on, says Lisa. You can set your income goal of $100,000, but without making a plan, how are you going to achieve that goal? The profit strategy is all about movement.

Always Keep Things Fresh

If you're not moving online, people won't see you. It's a psychological phenomenon, but it's true. Lisa explains that it's similar to when you're driving: You hardly notice the trees because they're still, but you notice a deer because it's moving. The same rules apply online.

You need to continuously give people fresh, new, exciting, and relevant content in order to capture their attention. If you don't, they'll cease to see you. So if your goal is to increase traffic in order to increase revenue, this is something important to keep in mind.

Turn Off Distractions

That being said, we can't spend all of our time online. Lisa talks a lot about "doing for doing sake"—in other words, doing things "just because" that aren't going to end up benefiting your business. Take social media, for example. We're all guilty of wasting far too much time on Twitter, Instagram, and all those other social outlets, but at the end of the day, they're just "pure fun," says Lisa.

In order to truly focus on your goals (especially when it comes to business) you must limit your distractions. There's always time for fun, afterward.

Celebrating Your Achieved Goals vs. Steps

Completion is key when setting your goals. Too often we can get caught up in celebrating the little steps we take along the way, but this can sometimes have a negative impact on our goals as a whole picture. Rewarding ourselves for the effort is fine, Lisa says, but the goal hasn't been achieved yet. We give ourselves pats on the back for projects that aren't complete, but until it is, should we really be celebrating?

This doesn't mean we should be too hard on ourselves, either. However, we should "get real about what's getting done" in terms of our goals. Every goal has strategies and plans behind it. But if you're celebrating every little step you take, what's going to be your motivation to finish?

Your goals are in your control. Inevitably, life will give you setbacks (the Internet will go down, your kids will get sick, you get behind on your daily plan) but you have to push through them to get to the final stages of your goal.

Taking a Break

It's okay to need a little refresher between goals. Lisa recalls challenging herself to go straight from one completed goal to starting a brand new one and finding herself caught up with emotional exhaustion and a devastated morale.

"Celebrating your goal by starting a new goal isn't a reward," she admits.

Sometimes your mind just needs some time off. That doesn't mean that you're not still being productive. You can chill out for a week, read books, and work on new strategies. But moving straight from one project to the next can prove to be exhausting—for anyone.

"I think it's important, especially for creatives, especially for creatives in business, to understand that need for release and allow it," Lisa says.

If you find yourself off-task or wandering away from your projects, just ask yourself: What can I do to give myself a break? Pushing yourself too far past your limits, of course, has negative impacts on your goals.

When you find yourself feeling this way—and chances are, you will—remember to ask yourself these questions:

- *What happened that broke me?*
- *Where did I push too hard?*
- *What did I finish and not allow myself a little release afterward?*
- *Whatever happened, what broke me, and how can I prevent this from happening again?*

Remember that it's okay to give yourself a little more leeway with your goals—especially your personal ones. There should be joy in your personal goals because "our lives are hard enough" and this should be fun.

Think about how you can infuse more joy into your daily goals. This isn't the time to be overly hard on yourself. When it comes to personal goals, Lisa's mantra is "Life should be loved, and lived, and energetic and alive."

lifestyle profile

I am a mother of four children. I've been married for a long time. I'm celebrating my 20th marriage anniversary this year. I got married when I was 19 years old. That is my personal side. My children are 15, 14, 10, and nine. I have two boys and two girls, a great family of six. We feel really big but we feel intimate at the same time—love that.

I started my business when my youngest two were still toddlers, and the whole goal of that was so that I could continue to be here on school holidays and summer vacations and sick days. Sick days are so important to me. When somebody doesn't feel good I don't have to worry about outside obligations. My workday consists of the hours that they are in school, and so I typically work from 8:30 to 2:30.

Favorite Hour of the Day

I think the hour 7:30 to 8:30 a.m. has to be my favorite because I've seen every member of my family, but I'm settling into my workday, so it's also very productive. I feel like I have a fresh slate every day and it's like there's so much potential in that time period of the day.

Sunday Soundtrack

Lately, I've been addicted to these like half-smutty, half-psychotic fiction novels by Colleen Hoover. I'm reading everything she's ever written. I start Sunday with some coffee, and usually I just can't—I mean my eyes aren't even open yet and I'm thinking about what's going to happen in those books. So, I guess my soundtrack is smutty and psychotic.

Most Admired Character Trait

My husband comes to mind because his work ethic. He just has this drive behind him, this ambition, and this duty to responsibility and what matters in his life—this duty to his priorities and his values, and I really admire that in people.

Business Background

I am a marketing strategist for online entrepreneurs. I love to help creative businesses, and when I say "creative" I think of anybody who's really carving their own path—people who are kind of stepping away from traditional careers and building something.

Think along the lines of passive income. Think along the lines of web forums and people contacting and ways you can work with a lot of people at one time. Online entrepreneurs, creative online entrepreneurs—I help them grow and profit online. One of my talents is helping people get to the next level in their business. It's very easy to get stuck in a rut, and I am a rut-buster when it comes to that kind of thing.

bio

Lisa Jacobs is a marketing consultant for creative entrepreneurs. Her expertise comes from her own success in turning $100 of supplies into thousands of sales and a top-earning Etsy® storefront. She freely shares her insights and strategy with like-minded entrepreneurial spirits on the blog Marketing Creativity and is the proud creator of The Luminaries Club: your creative business headquarters.

AFTERWORD

Reflection & Journal Questions

Make plans.
Work the plan.
Achieve the dream.

We hope that you're encouraged to start planning and stick to a practice that works for you. What we've learned from the process of writing this book is that there are many ways to set goals. The main takeaway, however, is that we all have to do it and in a way that doesn't feel restrictive. It should help you to reach new heights because your goals are worth planning for.

Use this chapter to do reflection and decide how you want to set your goals.. We asked all of our contributors why they plan. We asked them to dig deep and tell us their fifth-layer reason for why they choose to plan. We'd love to hear your answer as well.

Here are some suggestions on how to use this chapter: Go through and answer the questions that resonate for you or ones you might usually avoid when sitting down to write down your goals. Find a biz buddy to meet up with to discuss your takeaways and do some planning with. Or organize a book club gathering to talk about whose profiles you resonated with and what ideas were sparked by their accounts.

No matter what you decide to do, we hope you'll take action. You've got big plans, and we can't wait to see them come to life.

Grab a pen and make your notes in the following pages or grab a separate notebook to write your thoughts in. Make a mess; get in there and make room in your life for all that you can imagine.

Reflection is the first tool in figuring out how to become a more effective planner. Just because you're constantly making a list doesn't mean you're effective at setting goals. Noticing the habits you have when you set your goals and how you create a plan of attack is the quickest way to get you closer to your goals.

Notice the fears that pop up as you think about what went well and what might have gone off course. **Be honest in your answers and gentle with yourself as you answer these questions.**

Reflection

How did the last year go?

What am I proud of in my business and in my life?

What do I want to see change? What am I tired of complaining or dreaming about?

Where did I feel really loved?

Who do I need to bring more of into my life?

Who do I want to be?

What did I expect I'd get done but didn't?

How am I feeling in my life right now?

What am I grateful for?

What can I celebrate?

Reflection for When the Goal Doesn't Happen

If I didn't achieve my goal, what progress did I make?

What do I need to call myself out on?

What did I get distracted by?

What is my tendency or habit when I don't meet a goal?
How would I like to act if I don't meet my goal?

Am I not motivated about this particular goal?

Have I lost sight of the why?

Am I just not connected to this goal? Is this actually not something that's important to me?

Did I know a goal didn't feel right and yet continue to chase it? Why?

What's the one pervasive story that keeps on coming up that keeps me from achieving my goals?

How did my fear impact the goal not getting accomplished? What is the fear I'm holding on to?

Goal Setting

How do I want to feel this year?

What are some things I'd like to accomplish in the next year? Next six months? Next quarter?

If I achieve this goal, what will happen as a result of it? Who will be impacted?

Lara Casey talked about setting more heart goals. What in my life could I set a heart goal around to see it come to fruition?

What are some business goals, life goals (family or home), and personal goals that I want to set?

Is my goal something that future generations will be proud of me for?

What do I want to be reviewing next year?

How can I use what I have to get to where I ultimately wanted to be?

Is this goal big enough? Too big?

What am I grateful for (and would like more of)?

What steps will I need to take to make this happen?

What are the tools/people/resources I need to make sure this happens?

Habits to Make Your Goal Stick

What are the weekly, monthly and daily things that I'm willing to do to make my goals stick?

What am I willing to give up to make sure my goal happens?

What behavioral changes do I need to make?

What are all the structural changes I need to make?

What are the mindset changes I need to make?

Where do I need to write down my plans so I remember what goals I set for myself?

Make a Declaration

This _____ (month/quarter/year), I'm going to _____ (your goal). This is important to me because _____ (why you'll pursue this goal). When I accomplish this goal, I'll celebrate by _____ (give yourself an incentive). I'm going to _____ (person or resource that will help you be accountable to your goal) to ensure I stick to my goal.

I plan because
_____
_____

Gratitude

We have so much gratitude for this book coming together. It was, like many of our goals, just a little spark of an idea to start. As we started to listen more intently to our friends, our clients, and our communities, we realized that this book needed to be released into the world. It couldn't just live inside us and our brilliant contributors.

Dannie

This book is a representation of so many wonderful things coming together seamlessly. A beautiful partnership with an incredibly talented co-writer. The amazing talents of 13 brilliant entrepreneurs. The guidance and support of a wonderful team. I am so grateful for the symmetry of all of these things and what we have created.

I am also grateful for the external support that makes projects like these possible. As always, my greatest cheerleaders: Mom, Granny, Grampy. You are my superhero team, ready to defend and protect. Sascha, You may be a recent addition to this loyal tribe, but i am grateful for Your guidance and unwavering support and confidence. May Your light continue to brighten my darkness and my light continue to soften Yours. To my entrepreneur squad, y'all are the ones that make coming to work worthwhile. You know who you are and I am grateful for you.

Reina

I've always been the binder-wielding, ultra type-A gal. Planning runs in my veins. It has always broken my heart to hear people say that they aren't good at it or that it doesn't work for them. This book is for the women whose dreams still rest inside her creative mind, yearning to be seen. Your dreams matter and they'll make world a better place.

Our incredible contributors: Tara Gentile. Natalie Franke. Lacey Sites. Lara Casey. Ashley and Graham Scobey. Amber McCue. Tara Newman. Courtney Johnston. Jillian Smith. Jenna Kutcher. Lisa Jacobs. Thank you for being a part of this book and lighting up the world with your leadership. I am grateful for your friendship.

Jodi Brandon, our fearless editor. You've led a hesitant writer with your firm hand in edits and with your gentle words. I felt so cared for in this process. I can't wait to do it again.

Dannie, my BPCM buddy, this collaboration is more than just a book coming together for me, and I'm so grateful for our work together and our growing friendship. Here's to more goals chased, more places seen, and fierceness wielded.

The Reina + Co Team, you drive this machine with me and I am so grateful. Rachel, Caitlyn, Kaitlyn, Melina, Illiah, Autumn, thank you for your support in making this book happen.

My friends in this crazy entrepreneur journey, I couldn't do this without your encouragement, random gifs, and Voxer messages to keep going.

GRATITUDE

To David, take each day with delight. For Cato, you light me up. Thank you for pushing me to make brave choices. Let's keep leaning into what we're called to do.

Made in United States
Troutdale, OR
06/07/2024